Emotionally Healthy Spirituality

Day by Day

Emotionally Healthy Spirituality
Day by Day

A 40-DAY JOURNEY *with the* DAILY OFFICE

Previously published as *The Daily Office*

Peter Scazzero

ZONDERVAN

Emotionally Healthy Spirituality Day by Day

Copyright © 2008, 2014 by Peter Scazzero

Previously published as *The Daily Office*

This title is also available as a Zondervan ebook.
Visit www.zondervan.com/ebooks.

Requests for information should be addressed to:

Zondervan, 3900 *Sparks Dr. SE, Grand Rapids, Michigan* 49546

ISBN 978-0-310-34116-1

Author is represented by Christopher Ferebee, Attorney and Literary Agent, www.christopherferebee.com

Cover design: AbneyRanville
Cover image: ©jgroup / iStockphoto®
Interior design: Katherine Lloyd, The DESK
Interior illustration: © iconeer / iStock®

First printing June 2014 / Printed in the United States of America

Contents

Acknowledgments

I want to thank Geri, my wife, my best friend, and my favorite companion in "The Journey." She has spent countless hours prayerfully pondering and experimenting with these Daily Offices in a variety of contexts. Her work crafting thoughtful questions is meant to touch the soul and lead us to a personal experience of God. What a gift!

Thank you.

Introduction

Most Christians today are struggling — especially when it comes to spending time with God. You may be one of them.

For more than twenty-seven years I have been a pastor in Queens, New York, of a large, urban church with people from over seventy-three nations. At the same time, I have traveled throughout the United States and Canada speaking to pastors and church leaders, observing the church in a variety of settings and denominations.

The following are my observations about the current spiritual condition of most of us in our churches today. We are

- living off of other people's spirituality.
- scattered, fragmented, and uncentered.
- physically, spiritually, and emotionally tired.
- existing with only a one-inch-deep spirituality.
- praying and communing with God very little.
- not very intentional in pursuing Jesus.
- feeling stuck in our spiritual journey with Christ.
- struggling to stop our "life on the run."

The purpose of this book is to introduce you to a revolutionary spiritual discipline called the "Daily Office." When crafted to fit our unique personalities, temperaments, life situations, and vocations, it offers us an anchor powerful enough to slow us down amid the unceasing demands of our lives.

The Daily Office differs from what we label today as "quiet time" or "devotions." Quiet time and devotions normally take place once a day, in the mornings, and emphasize "getting filled up for the day" or "interceding for the needs around me." The Daily Office normally takes place at least twice a day, and is not so much a turning to God to *get* something; it is about *being with God* — about communion with him.[1]

The goal of the Daily Office, as with a "quiet time," is to pay attention to God throughout the entire day while I am active. This is the great challenge for all of us. Both the enormous pressure of the world, with the demonic powers behind it, and our own stubborn self-wills make it easy to live most of our waking hours without any consistent awareness of God's presence.

The word *office* comes from the Latin word *opus*, or "work." For the early church, the Daily Office was always the "work of God." Nothing was to interfere with that priority.

King David, three thousand years ago, understood this. He practiced set times of prayer seven times a day (Psalm 119:164). Daniel prayed three times a day (Daniel 6:10). Devout Jews in Jesus' time prayed at fixed hours — morning, afternoon, and evening. These set times of prayer were one of the Israelites' great treasures, providing a way to keep their lives centered on the invitation to love God with all their hearts, minds, soul, and strength. Even after Jesus' resurrection, his disciples continued to pray at certain hours of the day (Acts 3:1; 10:2 – 23).

About AD 525, a good man named Benedict structured these prayer times around eight Daily Offices, including one for monks in the middle of the night. He wrote the Rule of St. Benedict for laymen, and its purpose was to set rules for domestic life so that one could live (as fully as possible) the type of life presented in the gospel. It was a means to the goodness of life. At one point in his Rule, Benedict wrote: "On hearing the signal for an hour of the divine office, the monk will immediately set aside what he has in hand and go with utmost speed. Indeed, nothing is to be preferred to the Work of God [that is, the Daily Office]."[2]

All of these people realized that stopping to be with God, by means of the Daily Office, was the key to creating a continual and easy familiarity with God's presence for the rest of the day. I know it does that for me.

The great power in setting apart small units of time for morning, midday, and evening prayer infuses the rest of my day's activities with a deep sense of the sacred — of God. I remember that all time is his. The Daily Office, when practiced consistently, works to eliminate the division of the sacred and the secular in our lives.

One of the great barriers for many of us in spending time alone with God is the lack of a flexible, balanced structure to guide us. This rendition of the Daily Office seeks to provide a means to serve you in your time with God. Remember, God has built each of us differently. What works for one person will not necessarily work for another.

Like any powerful tool or discipline, the Daily Office can easily become a new legalism. For this reason, I have provided only two Daily Offices per day (one to be done morning or midday and the other for midday or evening). You may, for example, do one in the morning and the other at midday, or you may do one at midday and the other in the evening before you go to bed.

You choose the length of time for your Offices. The key, remember, is the regular remembrance of God, not the length of time. Your pausing to be with God can last anywhere from two minutes to twenty minutes to forty-five minutes. My wife, Geri, and I choose to have longer times with God in the mornings and then shorter ones at midday and in the evenings. It is up to you.

The following are the five elements contained in each Office in this book:

1. Silence, Stillness, and Centering

This is the essence of a Daily Office. We stop our activity and pause to be with the Living God. Scripture commands us: "Be still before the LORD and wait patiently for him" (Psalm 37:7), and "Be still, and know that I am God" (Psalm 46:10). We move into God's presence and rest there; that alone is no small feat. There are times when I pause for my midday prayer and find that I spend the entire time available — be it five or twenty minutes — centering so I can let go of my tensions, distractions, and sensations and begin resting in the love of God.

Each Office begins and ends with two minutes of silence. All religions practice silence. What makes silence unique for *us* is that we are silent before the *Lord* himself. This will be difficult, especially at first. Our internal and external worlds are filled with noise and distractions. For this reason, silence is probably the most challenging and least experienced discipline among Christians today. Give yourself lots of grace here. Studies suggest that the average person or group can only bear fifteen seconds of silence.

2. Scripture

The important thing to remember here is "less is more." I have limited the amount of Scripture for each Office. Read slowly — aloud if possible — chewing on different words or phrases. If God leads you to stop on a verse, do so. Be attentive in your heart to what God is doing inside of you. There is no need to finish all that is provided for each Office! Allow the Holy Spirit to guide you.

3. Devotional Reading

The purpose of these devotionals is to stretch you in your journey. I have integrated riches from a wide variety of sources — ancient spiritual writers, poetry, monks, Hasidic Jewish rabbis, and modern literature, as well as themes from my own book *Emotionally Healthy Spirituality* — and connected them to the Scripture reading. These devotionals are meant to be read slowly and prayerfully. There are times when I come to the midday or evening Office with so much on my mind that I begin with the devotional reading so that I can stop and center. Sometimes the devotionals will speak powerfully to where you are. God may lead you to ponder and meditate on a particular sentence or paragraph. At other times, you may want to skip them altogether. Again, remember, the purpose of the Daily Office is to commune with God, not to get though all that is written!

4. Question to Consider

Each devotion ends with a question to consider. I have written the questions to be brief but probing. You may find it helpful to write out your answers to God. Don't be surprised if God leads you along very different paths with these questions each time you repeat the study. Or feel free to skip them if they are not helpful.

5. Prayer

For a large part of my Christian life, I was against written prayers. In recent years, however, I have found them to be a rich supplement to my devotional life. You may want to pray the words as written, or just use them as inspiration and pray your own words. Again, use them only if they are helpful.

I have written *Emotionally Healthy Spirituality Day by Day* for small groups, Sunday school classes, and churches doing *The EHS Course* (*The Emotionally Healthy Spirituality Course*).[3] Each week's theme is based on a chapter from my book *Emotionally Healthy Spirituality*. If you are not in a group, you are strongly encouraged to read the designated chapters for each week's study. This will acquaint you with its profound themes and allow you to integrate them more effectively. I've also realized in writing this book that it provides an accessible introduction to a spiritual life shaped by the powerful rhythms of the Daily Office — regardless of whether the person has read the book or participated in a group studying the workbook.

The Lord's Prayer is included in appendix A as an additional aid in your time with God. Because of both its depth and simplicity, I often pray it as part of my Daily Offices each day.

A Word to Groups

While these Daily Offices have been written for individuals, they can also be adapted for groups meeting for morning, midday, or evening prayer. My recommendations for those who do this are as follows:

- Appoint a facilitator to pace the time.
- Read the Scripture and final written prayers aloud together.

- Appoint one person to read the devotional aloud for the group.
- Pause for five to fifteen seconds between the reading and the prayer.

A Final Exhortation

Remember, the Daily Offices are about creating a rhythm of stopping to be with God at set times each day in order to cultivate our personal relationship with him throughout the day — that we might prefer the love of Christ above all else.

Keep clearly in mind that whether you have been a Christian praying for fifty years or for only one week, we are all beginners at prayer. This is not about "doing it right" or tying you down to a legalistic schedule. Remember what the apostle Paul wrote: "Therefore do not let anyone judge you by what you eat or drink, or with regard to a religious festival, a New Moon celebration or a Sabbath day [or a Daily Office]. These are a shadow of the things that were to come; the reality, however, is found in Christ" (Colossians 2:16 – 17).

The Problem of Emotionally Unhealthy Spirituality

DAY 1: MORNING/MIDDAY OFFICE

Silence, Stillness, and Centering before God (2 minutes)

Scripture Reading: Mark 11:15 – 17

> On reaching Jerusalem, Jesus entered the temple courts and began driving out those who were buying and selling there. He overturned the tables of the money changers and the benches of those selling doves, and would not allow anyone to carry merchandise through the temple courts. And as he taught them, he said, "Is it not written: 'My house will be called a house of prayer for all nations'? But you have made it 'a den of robbers.'"

Devotional

Jesus' intense anger and overturning of the tables in the temple courts ought to make us gasp. He knows that if we don't get to God, invaluable treasures will be lost or obscured. We lose the space where we experience God's unfailing love and amazing forgiveness. We lose an eternal perspective on what is important and what is not. We lose compassion. We gain the world but lose our souls (Mark 8:36 – 37).

Be Free for God
I have a need
of such clearance
as the Savior effected in the temple of Jerusalem
a riddance of clutter
of what is secondary
that blocks the way

19

> to the all-important central emptiness
> which is filled
> with the presence of God alone.
> — Jean Danielou[4]

Question to Consider

How would you describe "what is secondary" in your life, the thing that might be "blocking the way" to experiencing God?

Prayer

> *Lord, help me to see how much I lose when I lose you. My perspective on my life and all of life gets distorted when I don't make space for you, obscuring your love for me. Your love is better than life, and truly I long for more tastes of that love. In Jesus' name, amen.*

Conclude with Silence (2 minutes)

DAY 1: MIDDAY/EVENING OFFICE

Silence, Stillness, and Centering before God (2 minutes)

Scripture Reading: 1 Samuel 15:22 – 23

But Samuel replied:

"Does the LORD delight in burnt offerings and sacrifices
    as much as in obeying the LORD?
To obey is better than sacrifice,
    and to heed is better than the fat of rams.
For rebellion is like the sin of divination,
    and arrogance like the evil of idolatry.
Because you have rejected the word of the LORD,
    he has rejected you as king."

Devotional

Saul, the first king of Israel, did not know much about silence or listening to God. Like David, he was a gifted, anointed, successful military/political leader. Yet unlike David, we never see him seeking to be with God. In this passage, Samuel the prophet reprimands Saul for doing many religious acts (i.e., offering burnt offerings and sacrifices) but not quieting himself enough to listen, or "to heed" God (v. 22).

> We all must take the time to be silent and to contemplate, especially those who live in big cities like London and New York, where everything moves so fast.... I always begin my prayer in silence, for it is in the silence of the heart that God speaks. God is the friend of silence — we need to listen to God because it's not what we say but what He says to us and through us that matters. Prayer feeds the soul — as blood is to the body, prayer is to the soul — and it brings you closer to God. It also gives you a clean and pure heart. A clean heart can see God, can speak to God, and can see the love of God in others.
>
> — Mother Teresa[5]

Question to Consider

How could you make more room in your life for silence in order to listen to God?

Prayer

Unclutter my heart, O God, until I am quiet enough to hear you speak out of the silence. Help me in these few moments to stop, to listen, to wait, to be still, and to allow your presence to envelop me. In Jesus' name, amen.

Conclude with Silence (2 minutes)

DAY 2: MORNING/MIDDAY OFFICE

Silence, Stillness, and Centering before God (2 minutes)

Scripture Reading: Jonah 1:1 – 4

> The word of the LORD came to Jonah son of Amittai: "Go to the great city of Nineveh and preach against it, because its wickedness has come up before me."
>
> But Jonah ran away from the LORD and headed for Tarshish. He went down to Joppa, where he found a ship bound for that port. After paying the fare, he went aboard and sailed for Tarshish to flee from the LORD.
>
> Then the LORD sent a great wind on the sea, and such a violent storm arose that the ship threatened to break up.

Devotional

Jonah is an example of a prophet with a case of emotionally unhealthy spirituality. He hears and serves God but refuses to listen to God's call to love and show mercy to Nineveh, a world power of that day known for its violent, barbaric behavior. Jonah flees 2,400 miles in the opposite direction, to Tarshish, in present-day Spain.

> And why Tarshish? For one thing, it is a lot more exciting than Nineveh. Nineveh was an ancient site with layer after layer of ruined and unhappy history. Going to Nineveh to preach was not a coveted assignment for a Hebrew prophet with good references. But Tarshish was something else. Tarshish was exotic. Tarshish was adventure.... Tarshish in the biblical references was a "far off and sometimes idealized port." It is reported in 1 Kings 10:22 that Solomon's fleet of Tarshish fetched gold,

silver, ivory, monkeys and peacocks.... In Tarshish we can have a religious career without having to deal with God.

— Eugene Peterson[6]

As Jonah runs, however, God sends a great storm. Jonah loses control of his life and destiny. He is thrown overboard and swallowed by a great fish. It is from the belly of the fish that Jonah begins to wrestle with God in prayer.

Question to Consider

What internal or external storm might God be sending into your life as a sign that something is not right spiritually?

Prayer

Lord, may your will, not my will, be done in my life. You know how easy it is to call myself a Christian but then become busy, forgetting about your will and desires. Forgive me for this sin. Help me listen to you, and grant me the courage to faithfully surrender to you. In Jesus' name, amen.

Conclude with Silence (2 minutes)

DAY 2: MIDDAY/EVENING OFFICE

Silence, Stillness, and Centering before God (2 minutes)

Scripture Reading: 1 John 2:15 – 17

Do not love the world or anything in the world. If anyone loves the world, love for the Father is not in them. For everything in the world — the lust of the flesh, the lust of the eyes, and the pride of life — comes not from the Father but from the world. The world and its desires pass away, but whoever does the will of God lives forever.

Devotional

At the end of the third century in the deserts of Egypt, an extraordinary phenomenon occurred. Christian men and women began to flee the cities and villages to see God in the desert. They discerned how easy it was to lose one's soul in the entanglements and manipulations found in society, so they pursued God in a radical way by moving to the desert. They became known as the "Desert Fathers."

> Society ... was regarded by them as a shipwreck from which each single individual man had to swim for his life.... These were men who believed that to let oneself drift along, passively accepting the tenets and values of what they knew as society, was purely and simply a disaster.... They knew they were helpless to do any good for others as long as they floundered about in the wreckage. But once they got a foothold on solid ground, things were different. Then they had not only the power but even the obligation to pull the whole world to safety after them.
>
> — Thomas Merton[7]

Question to Consider

How do you hear the words of the apostle John today: "Do not love the world or anything in the world" (1 John 2:15)?

Prayer

Lord, in order to be with you, I need you to show me how to "create a desert" in the midst of my full, active life. Cleanse me from the pressures, illusions, and pretenses that confront me today so that my life may serve as a gift to those around me.

Conclude with Silence (2 minutes)

DAY 3: MORNING/MIDDAY OFFICE

Silence, Stillness, and Centering before God (2 minutes)

Scripture Reading: Genesis 32:22 – 26, 30

That night Jacob got up and took his two wives, his two female servants and his eleven sons and crossed the ford of the Jabbok. After he had sent them across the stream, he sent over all his possessions. So Jacob was left alone, and a man wrestled with him till daybreak. When the man saw that he could not overpower him, he touched the socket of Jacob's hip so that his hip was wrenched as he wrestled with the man. Then the man said, "Let me go, for it is daybreak." But Jacob replied, "I will not let you go unless you bless me."

So Jacob called the place Peniel, saying, "It is because I saw God face to face, and yet my life was spared."

Devotional

Jacob's name can mean "cheat" or "grabber," and he lived up to his name. He was manipulative, deceptive, and aggressive — not someone you'd likely nominate for a leadership position in your church. Jacob was a seriously flawed person growing up in a dysfunctional family. He seemed to be either getting into trouble, just getting out of it, or about to make some more.[8]

Jacob's story is so universal because it is so personal. Throughout his life, Jacob was stubborn and unwilling to trust anyone — even God. It was at the Jabbok brook that Jacob was finally broken by God and radically transformed. He was given a new name and a new freedom to live as God originally intended. This came, however, at the price of a permanent limp that rendered him helpless and desperate to cling to God. And it is out of this weak place of dependence that Jacob became a nation (Israel) that would bless the world.

In the same way, God sometimes wounds us in our journey with him in order to move us out of an unhealthy, "tip of the iceberg" spirituality to one that truly transforms us from the inside out. When these wounds come, we can deny them, cover them, get angry with God, blame others, or like Jacob we can cling desperately to God.

Question to Consider
In what way(s) has God put your life or plans "out of joint" so that you might depend on him?

Prayer
Father, I relate to Jacob in striving, manipulating, scheming, denying, and spinning half- truths to those around me in order to get my way. At times, I too find myself serving you in order to get something from you. Lord, I invite you to teach me to live in dependence on you. Help me to rest and be still in your love alone. In Jesus' name, amen.

Conclude with Silence (2 minutes)

DAY 3: MIDDAY/EVENING OFFICE

Silence, Stillness, and Centering before God (2 minutes)

Scripture Reading: Matthew 16:21 – 23
From that time on Jesus began to explain to his disciples that he must go to Jerusalem and suffer many things at the hands of the elders, the chief priests and the teachers of the law, and that he must be killed and on the third day be raised to life.

Peter took him aside and began to rebuke him. "Never, Lord!" he said. "This shall never happen to you!"

Jesus turned and said to Peter, "Get behind me, Satan! You are a stumbling block to me; you do not have in mind the concerns of God, but merely human concerns."

Devotional

The apostle Peter had a passionate heart for Jesus, but he was also rash, proud, immature, and inconsistent. His impulsiveness and stubbornness are evident throughout the gospels.

Yet Jesus patiently led Peter to a crucifixion of his self-will, in order that he might experience genuine resurrection life and power.

When I am still, compulsion (the busyness that Hilary of Tours called "a blasphemous anxiety to do God's work for him") gives way to compunction (being pricked or punctured). That is, God can break through the many layers with which I protect myself, so that I can hear his Word and be poised to listen....

In perpetual motion I can mistake the flow of my adrenaline for the moving of the Holy Spirit; I can live in the illusion that I am ultimately in control of my destiny and my daily affairs....

French philosopher and mathematician Blaise Pascal observed that most of our human problems come because we don't know how to sit still in our room for an hour.

— Leighton Ford[9]

Question to Consider

What might be one way your busyness blocks you from listening and communing intimately with the living God?

Prayer

Lord, forgive me for running my life without you today. I offer my anxieties to you now — as best I can. Help me to be still, to surrender to your will, and to rest in your loving arms. In the name of the Father, the Son, and the Holy Spirit, amen.

Conclude with Silence (2 minutes)

DAY 4: MORNING/MIDDAY OFFICE

Silence, Stillness, and Centering before God (2 minutes)

Scripture Reading: Luke 10:38 – 42

As Jesus and his disciples were on their way, he came to a village where a woman named Martha opened her home to him. She had a sister called Mary, who sat at the Lord's feet listening to what he said. But Martha was distracted by all the preparations that had to be made. She came to him and asked, "Lord, don't you care that my sister has left me to do the work by myself? Tell her to help me!"

"Martha, Martha," the Lord answered, "you are worried and upset about many things, but few things are needed — or indeed only one. Mary has chosen what is better, and it will not be taken away from her."

Devotional

Mary and Martha represent two approaches to the Christian life.

Martha is actively serving Jesus, but she is also missing Jesus. She is busy in the "doing" of life. Her life is pressured and filled with distractions. Her duties have become disconnected from her love for Jesus. Martha's problems, however, go beyond her busyness. I suspect that if Martha were to sit at the feet of Jesus, she would still be distracted by everything on her mind. Her inner person is touchy, irritable, and anxious.

Mary, on the other hand, is sitting at the feet of Jesus, listening to him. She is "being" with Jesus, enjoying intimacy with him, loving him, and taking pleasure in his presence. Her life has one center of gravity — Jesus. I suspect that if Mary were to help with the many household chores, she would not be worried or upset. Why? Her inner person has slowed down enough to focus on Jesus and to center her life on him.

Our goal is to love God with our whole being, to be consistently conscious of God through our daily life — whether we are stopped like Mary, sitting at the feet of Jesus, or active like Martha, taking care of the tasks of life.[10]

Question to Consider

What things are worrying or upsetting you today?

Prayer

Help me, O Lord, to be still and wait patiently for you (Psalm 37:7). I offer to you each of my anxieties and worries this day. Teach me to be prayerfully attentive and to rest in you as I enter into the many activities of this day. In Jesus' name, amen.

Conclude with Silence (2 minutes)

DAY 4: MIDDAY/EVENING OFFICE

Silence, Stillness, and Centering before God (2 minutes)

Scripture Reading: Psalm 62:5 – 8

Find rest, O my soul, in God alone;
    my hope comes from him.

29

He alone is my rock and my salvation;
  he is my fortress, I will not be shaken.
My salvation and my honor depend on God;
  he is my mighty rock, my refuge.
Trust in him at all times, O people;
  pour out your hearts to him,
  for God is our refuge. (NIV 1984)

Devotional

David, a man after God's own heart, beautifully models the seamless integration of a full emotional life with a profound contemplative life with God. He trusts in the Lord, pouring out his struggles, fears, and anguish over the lies being said about him.

In *The Cry of the Soul*, Dan Allender and Tremper Longman summarize why awareness of our feelings is so important to our relationship with God:

> Ignoring our emotions is turning our back on reality; listening to our emotions ushers us into reality. And reality is where we meet God.... Emotions are the language of the soul. They are the cry that gives the heart a voice.... However, we often turn a deaf ear — through emotional denial, distortion, or disengagement. We strain out anything disturbing in order to gain tenuous control of our inner world. We are frightened and ashamed of what leaks into our consciousness. In neglecting our intense emotions, we are false to ourselves and lose a wonderful opportunity to know God. We forget that change comes through brutal honesty and vulnerability before God.[11]

Question to Consider

What are you angry about today? Sad about? Afraid of? Pour out your response before God, trusting in him as David did.

Prayer

*Lord, like David I often feel like a leaning wall, a tottering fence
that is about to be knocked down! So many forces and circumstances seem to be coming against me. Help me, Lord, to find rest
in you and to take shelter in you as my fortress. In Jesus' name,
amen.*

Conclude with Silence (2 minutes)

DAY 5: MORNING/MIDDAY OFFICE

Silence, Stillness, and Centering before God (2 minutes)

Scripture Reading: John 7:2 – 8

But when the Jewish Festival of Tabernacles was near, Jesus'
brothers said to him, "Leave Galilee and go to Judea, so that
your disciples there may see the works you do. No one who
wants to become a public figure acts in secret. Since you are
doing these things, show yourself to the world." For even his
own brothers did not believe in him.

Therefore Jesus told them, "My time is not yet here; for you
any time will do. The world cannot hate you, but it hates me
because I testify that its works are evil. You go to the festival.
I am not yet going up to this festival, because my time has not
yet fully come."

Devotional

Jesus moved slowly, not striving or rushing. He patiently waited
through his adolescent and young adult years to reveal himself
as the Messiah. Even then, he did not rush to be recognized. He
waited patiently for his Father's timing during his short ministry.

Why is it then that we hate "slow" when God appears to delight in it? Eugene Peterson offers us at least two reasons:

> *I am busy because I am vain.* I want to appear important. Significant. What better way than to be busy? The incredible hours, the crowded schedule, and the heavy demands of my time are proof to myself — and to all who will notice — that I am important. If I go into a doctor's office and find there's no one waiting, and I see through a half-open door the doctor reading a book, I wonder if he's any good....
>
> Such experiences affect me. I live in a society in which crowded schedules and harassed conditions are evidence of importance, so I develop a crowded schedule and harassed conditions. When others notice, they acknowledge my significance, and my vanity is fed.
>
> *I am busy because I am lazy.* I indolently let others decide what I will do instead of resolutely deciding myself. It was a favorite theme of C. S. Lewis that only lazy people work hard. By lazily abdicating the essential work of deciding and directing, establishing values and setting goals, other people do it for us.[12]

Question to Consider

What is one step you can take today to slow down and live more attentively to the voice of Jesus?

Prayer

Lord, grant me the grace to do one thing at a time today, without rushing or hurrying. Help me to savor the sacred in all I do, be it large or small. By the Holy Spirit within me, empower me to pause today as I move from one activity to the next. In Jesus' name, amen.

Conclude with Silence (2 minutes)

DAY 5: MIDDAY/EVENING OFFICE

Silence, Stillness, and Centering before God (2 minutes)

Scripture Reading: 2 Corinthians 12:7 – 10

> Therefore, in order to keep me from becoming conceited, I was given a thorn in my flesh, a messenger of Satan, to torment me. Three times I pleaded with the Lord to take it away from me. But he said to me, "My grace is sufficient for you, for my power is made perfect in weakness." Therefore I will boast all the more gladly about my weaknesses, so that Christ's power may rest on me. That is why, for Christ's sake, I delight in weaknesses, in insults, in hardships, in persecutions, in difficulties. For when I am weak, then I am strong.

Devotional

The Bible does not spin the flaws and weaknesses of its heroes. Abraham lied. Hosea's wife was a prostitute. Peter rebuked God! Noah got drunk. Jonah was a racist. Jacob lied. John Mark deserted Paul. Elijah burned out. Jeremiah was depressed and suicidal. Thomas doubted. Moses had a temper. Timothy had ulcers. Even David, one of God's beloved friends, committed adultery with Bathsheba and murdered her husband. Yet all these people teach us the same message: that every human being on earth, regardless of their gifts and strengths, is weak, vulnerable, and dependent on God and others.[13]

The pressure to present an image of ourselves as strong and spiritually "together" hovers over most of us. We feel guilty for not measuring up, for not making the grade. We forget that all of us are human and frail.

The apostle Paul struggled with God not answering his prayers and removing his "thorn in the flesh." Nevertheless, he thanked God for his brokenness, knowing that without it, he would have been an arrogant, "conceited" apostle. He learned, as we all must, that Christ's power is made perfect only when we are weak.

Question to Consider

How might brokenness or weakness in your life today present an opportunity for God's power to be demonstrated?

Prayer

Father, the notion of admitting to myself and to others my weaknesses and failures is very difficult. Lord, I am weak. I am dependent on you. You are God, and I am not. Help me to embrace your work in me. And may I be able to say, like Paul, "when I am weak (broken), then I am strong." In Jesus' name, amen.

Conclude with Silence (2 minutes)

Know Yourself
That You May
Know God

DAILY OFFICES

Week Two

DAY 1: MORNING/MIDDAY OFFICE

Silence, Stillness, and Centering before God (2 minutes)

Scripture Reading: Mark 1:33 – 38

The whole town gathered at the door, and Jesus healed many who had various diseases. He also drove out many demons, but he would not let the demons speak because they knew who he was.

Very early in the morning, while it was still dark, Jesus got up, left the house and went off to a solitary place, where he prayed. Simon and his companions went to look for him, and when they found him, they exclaimed: "Everyone is looking for you!"

Jesus replied, "Let us go somewhere else — to the nearby villages — so I can preach there also. That is why I have come."

Devotional

The challenge to shed our "old false" self in order to live authentically in our "new true" self strikes at the very core of true spirituality. We see this authenticity in the life of Jesus.

In the midst of a mini-revival in the town of Capernaum, Jesus was able to withstand the pressure of everyone looking for him, and to move on to another place. He also knew his Father, who loved him and had a work for him to complete. In living faithfully to his true self, however, Jesus disappointed a lot of people. For example:

- He disappointed his family to the point where his mother and siblings wondered if he was out of his mind (Mark 3:21).

- He disappointed the people he grew up with in Nazareth. When Jesus declared who he really was — the Messiah — they tried to push him off a cliff (Luke 4:28 – 29).

- He disappointed his closest friends, the twelve disciples. They projected onto Jesus their own picture of the kind of Messiah they expected him to be. When he failed to meet their expectations, they quit on him.
- He disappointed the crowds. They wanted an earthly Messiah who would feed them, fix all their problems, overthrow the Roman oppressors, work miracles, and give inspiring sermons. They walked away from him.
- He disappointed the religious leaders. They did not appreciate the disruption his presence brought to their day-to-day lives or to their theology. They finally attributed his power to demons and had him crucified.[14]

Question to Consider

What might be one specific way that you give in to the expectations of others rather than being faithful to what Jesus has for you?

Prayer

Jesus, I am so grateful that you understand what it is like to feel pressure from the expectations of others. It can feel crushing at times. Lord, help me to love others well while at the same time remaining faithful to you. In Jesus' name, amen.

Conclude with Silence (2 minutes)

DAY 1: MIDDAY/EVENING OFFICE

Silence, Stillness, and Centering before God (2 minutes)

Scripture Reading: 1 Samuel 17:38–40, 45

Then Saul dressed David in his own tunic. He put a coat of armor on him and a bronze helmet on his head. David fastened on his sword over the tunic and tried walking around, because he was not used to them.

"I cannot go in these," he said to Saul, "because I am not used to them." So he took them off. Then he took his staff in his hand, chose five smooth stones from the stream, put them in the pouch of his shepherd's bag and, with his sling in his hand, approached the Philistine.

David said to the Philistine, "You come against me with sword and spear and javelin, but I come against you in the name of the LORD Almighty, the God of the armies of Israel, whom you have defied."

Devotional

Even as a young man, David knew both himself and God. Having taken off Saul's armor, he went up against the nine-foot Goliath with only his slingshot and a few smooth stones, confident in the living God.

Unlike David, however, the vast majority of us go to our graves without ever really knowing who we are. We unconsciously live someone else's life, or at least someone else's expectations for us.

We are so unaccustomed to being our true self that it can seem impossible to know where to begin. Thomas Merton describes what we so often do:

I use up my life in the desire for pleasures ... power, honor, knowledge and love, to clothe this false self.... And I wind experiences around myself and cover myself with pleasures and glory like bandages in order to make myself perceptible to myself and to the world, as if I were an invisible body that could only become visible when something visible covered its surface. But there is no substance under the things with which I am clothed. I am hollow, and my structure of pleasures and ambitions has no foundation.... And when they are gone there will be nothing left of me but my own nakedness and emptiness and hollowness.[15]

The path we must walk to remove the layers of our false self is initially very hard. Powerful forces around and inside us can smother the process. At the same time, the God of the universe has made his home in us (John 14:23), and the very glory God gave Jesus has also been given to us (John 17:21 – 23).

Question to Consider

What might be one false layer or bandage God is inviting you to remove today?

Prayer

Lord, grant me the courage of David to resist the temptation to live a life that is not the one you have given to me. Deliver me from the "Goliaths" in front of me, and from the negative voices I hear so often. Help me to listen and obey your voice today. In Jesus' name, amen.

Conclude with Silence (2 minutes)

DAY 2: MORNING/MIDDAY OFFICE

Silence, Stillness, and Centering before God (2 minutes)

Scripture Reading: Psalm 139:13 – 16

For you created my inmost being;
    you knit me together in my mother's womb.
I praise you because I am fearfully and wonderfully made;

your works are wonderful,
    I know that full well.
My frame was not hidden from you
    when I was made in the secret place,
    when I was woven together in the depths of the earth.
Your eyes saw my unformed body;
    all the days ordained for me were written in your book
    before one of them came to be.

Devotional

David seems to have maintained the tension of two complementary truths taught in Scripture. We are sinners who desperately need forgiveness and a Savior. At the same time, God created us in his image, knit each of us together in our mother's womb with enormous care, and chose us for a special purpose on earth. Parker Palmer captured well the wonder of Psalm 139:

> Vocation does not come from a voice "out there" calling me to become something I am not. It comes from a voice "in here" calling me to be the person I was born to be, to fulfill the original selfhood given me at birth by God.
>
> It is a strange gift, this birthright of self. Accepting it turns out to be even more demanding than attempting to become someone else! I have sometimes responded to that demand by ignoring the gift, or hiding it, or fleeing from it, or squandering it — and I think I am not alone. There is a Hasidic tale that reveals, with amazing brevity, both the universal tendency to want to be someone else and the ultimate importance of becoming one's self. Rabbi Zusya, when he was an old man, said, "In the coming world, they will not ask me: 'Why were you not Moses?' They will ask me: 'Why were you not Zusya?'"[16]

Question to Consider

What do you think might be one of your "birthright" gifts from God that you have ignored in your life?

Prayer

Lord, I come this day inviting you to cut those deeply entrenched chains that keep me from being faithful to my true self in Christ. In doing so, may my life be a blessing to many. In Jesus' name, amen.

Conclude with Silence (2 minutes)

DAY 2: MIDDAY/EVENING OFFICE

Silence, Stillness, and Centering before God (2 minutes)

Scripture Reading: Ephesians 3:14 – 19

For this reason I kneel before the Father, from whom every family in heaven and on earth derives its name. I pray that out of his glorious riches he may strengthen you with power through his Spirit in your inner being, so that Christ may dwell in your hearts through faith. And I pray that you, being rooted and established in love, may have power, together with all the Lord's holy people, to grasp how wide and long and high and deep is the love of Christ, and to know this love that surpasses knowledge — that you may be filled to the measure of all the fullness of God.

Devotional

Bernard of Clairvaux (AD 1090 – 1153), the abbot of a Cistercian monastery in France, was perhaps the greatest Christian leader and writer of his day. In his great work entitled *Loving God*, Bernard describes four degrees of love:

1. Loving ourselves for our own sake
2. Loving God for his gifts and blessings
3. Loving God for himself alone
4. Loving ourselves for the sake of God

The highest degree of love, for Bernard, was simply that we love ourselves as God loves us — in the same degree, in the same manner, and with the very same love. We love the self that God loves, the essential image and likeness of God in us that has been damaged by sin.[17]

Question to Consider

Where do you see yourself on Bernard's list of the four degrees of love?

Prayer

Lord, strengthen me with your power that I might grasp how wide and long and high and deep is the love of Christ that surpasses human knowledge. May I love you for you alone, and not your gifts or blessings. And may I live in the deep experience of your tender love this day. In Jesus' name, amen.

Conclude with Silence (2 minutes)

DAY 3: MORNING/MIDDAY OFFICE

Silence, Stillness, and Centering before God (2 minutes)

Scripture Reading: Mark 10:26 – 31

The disciples were even more amazed, and said to each other, "Who then can be saved?" Jesus looked at them and said, "With man this is impossible, but not with God; all things are possible with God." Then Peter spoke up, "We have left everything to follow you!"

"Truly I tell you," Jesus replied, "no one who has left home or brothers or sisters or mother or father or children or fields for me and the gospel will fail to receive a hundred times as much in this present age: homes, brothers, sisters, mothers, children and fields — along with persecutions — and in the age to come eternal life. But many who are first will be last, and the last first."

Devotional

Anthony (AD 251 – 356) grew up in a wealthy family in Egypt, receiving an excellent education and upbringing from his Christian parents. One Sunday, Anthony heard the words: "Go sell all you have and give it to the poor, and you shall have treasure in heaven," and he felt God speaking directly to his heart. Unlike the rich young ruler, he responded to Jesus in faith.

Selling his possessions, Anthony went off into the solitude of the Egyptian desert, not just for a few days or weeks, but for twenty years! He renounced all possessions to learn detachment; he renounced speech in order to learn compassion; and he renounced activity in order to learn prayer. In the desert, Anthony both discovered God and did intense battle with the devil.

When Anthony emerged from his solitude after twenty years, people recognized in him the qualities of an authentic "healthy" man — whole in body, mind, and soul. God soon catapulted him into one of the most remarkable ministries of that day. He preached the gospel among the rich and the poor, performed many healings, expelled demons, and more. Emperor Constantine Augustus sought out Anthony's counsel. He served tirelessly in prisons and among the poor.[18]

In his old age, Anthony retired to an even deeper solitude to be totally absorbed in direct communion with God. He died in the year 356 at the age of 106 years old.[19]

Question to Consider

What impresses you most about the story of Anthony's life?

Prayer

Lord, it is clear that layers of Anthony's false, superficial self were shed during his time with you. Crack the hard shell over my heart that obscures and buries my true self in Christ. Transform me into the kind of person you desire me to be. In Jesus' name, amen.

Conclude with Silence (2 minutes)

DAY 3: MIDDAY/EVENING OFFICE

Silence, Stillness, and Centering before God (2 minutes)

Scripture Reading: Matthew 4:1 – 3, 8 – 11

Then Jesus was led by the Spirit into the desert to be tempted by the devil. After fasting forty days and forty nights, he was hungry. The tempter came to him and said, "If you are the Son of God, tell these stones to become bread."

Again, the devil took him to a very high mountain and showed him all the kingdoms of the world and their splendor. "All this I will give you," he said, "if you will bow down and worship me."

Jesus said to him, "Away from me, Satan! For it is written: 'Worship the Lord your God, and serve him only.'" Then the devil left him, and angels came and attended him.

Devotional

Solitude is the furnace of transformation. Without solitude we remain victims of our society and continue to be entangled in the illusions of the false self. Jesus himself entered into this furnace. There he was tempted with the three compulsions of the world: to be relevant ("turn stones into loaves"), to be spectacular ("throw yourself down"), and to be powerful ("I will give you all these kingdoms"). There he affirmed God as the only source of his identity ("You must worship the Lord your God and serve him alone"). Solitude is the place of the great struggle and the great encounter — the struggle against the compulsions of the false self, and the encounter with the loving God who offers himself as the substance of the new self. . . .

In solitude I get rid of my scaffolding: no friends to talk with, no telephone calls to make. . . . The task is to persevere in my solitude, to stay in my cell until all my seductive visitors get tired of pounding on my door and leave me alone.

— Henri Nouwen[20]

Question to Consider

What temptations or trials do you find yourself in today that God might be using as a furnace to help develop your interior life?

Prayer

Lord, help me to turn down the volume of the voices that tell me I have little worth unless I am wealthy, influential, and popular. Grant me the grace today to experience your voice, which tells me: You are "my [child], whom I love; with [you] I am well pleased" (Matthew 3:16). In Jesus' name, amen.

Conclude with Silence (2 minutes)

DAY 4: MORNING/MIDDAY OFFICE

Silence, Stillness, and Centering before God (2 minutes)

Scripture Reading: 1 Kings 19:1 – 5

Now Ahab told Jezebel everything Elijah had done and how he had killed all the prophets with the sword. So Jezebel sent a messenger to Elijah to say, "May the gods deal with me, be it ever so severely, if by this time tomorrow I do not make your life like that of one of them."

Elijah was afraid and ran for his life. When he came to Beersheba in Judah, he left his servant there, while he himself went a day's journey into the wilderness. He came to a broom bush, sat down under it and prayed that he might die. "I have had enough, LORD," he said. "Take my life; I am no better than my ancestors." Then he lay down under the bush and fell asleep.

All at once an angel touched him and said, "Get up and eat."

Devotional

After Elijah's great victory over 850 false prophets at Mount Carmel, he had to run for his life. During that process, he became both exhausted and depressed — to the point of wanting to die. For reasons not given in this text, we find Elijah alone under a broom bush and asking for death. He is, as we call it today, "burned out."

When I give something I do not possess, I give a false and dangerous gift, a gift that looks like love but is, in reality, loveless — a gift given more from my need to prove myself than from the other's need to be cared for....

One sign that I am violating my own nature in the name of nobility is a condition called burnout. Though usually regarded as the result of trying to give too much, burnout in my experience results from trying to give what I do not possess — the ultimate in giving too little! Burnout is a state of emptiness, to be sure, but it does not result from giving all I have; it merely reveals the nothingness from which I was trying to give in the first place.

— Parker Palmer[21]

Question to Consider

What would it look like for you to respect yourself in light of your God-given human limits?

Prayer

Jesus, you know my tendency to say yes to more commitments than I can possibly keep. Help me to embrace the gift of my limits physically, emotionally, and spiritually. And may you, Lord Jesus, be glorified in and through me today. In your name, amen.

Conclude with Silence (2 minutes)

DAY 4: MIDDAY/EVENING OFFICE

Silence, Stillness, and Centering before God (2 minutes)

Scripture Reading: Exodus 3:1 – 5

Now Moses was tending the flock of Jethro his father-in-law, the priest of Midian, and he led the flock to the far side of the wilderness and came to Horeb, the mountain of God. There the angel of the LORD appeared to him in flames of fire from within a bush. Moses saw that though the bush was on fire it did not burn up. So Moses thought, "I will go over and see this strange sight — why the bush does not burn up."

When the LORD saw that he had gone over to look, God called to him from within the bush, "Moses! Moses!"

And Moses said, "Here I am."

"Do not come any closer," God said. "Take off your sandals, for the place where you are standing is holy ground."

Devotional

God's presence in us is like the fire in the Burning Bush. It gradually takes us over, so that although we remain fully ourselves, we are being made over into our true selves, the way God originally intended us to be. He is Light, and we are filled with His light — maybe even literally, as some saints were said to visibly glow. The term for this transformation is fairly scandalizing: *theosis*, which means being transformed into God, divinized or deified. Of course we do not become little mini-gods with our own universes. We never lose our identity, but we are filled with God like a sponge is filled with water.

— Frederica Mathewes-Green[22]

Question to Consider

What is one area of your inner person that the fire of God's presence might want to burn away (e.g., selfishness, greed, bitterness, impatience)?

Prayer

Jesus, I believe that you came to save me from the penalty of my sins — death — and for eternal life. At the same time, you came to save me from the poison that flows in my veins, from that which keeps me from your Light. Come invade me with your burning fire that I might become the person you have created me to be in you. In your name, amen.

Conclude with Silence (2 minutes)

DAY 5: MORNING/MIDDAY OFFICE

Silence, Stillness, and Centering before God (2 minutes)

Scripture Reading: Romans 8:35 – 39

Who shall separate us from the love of Christ? Shall trouble or hardship or persecution or famine or nakedness or danger or sword? As it is written:

"For your sake we face death all day long;
we are considered as sheep to be slaughtered."

No, in all these things we are more than conquerors through him who loved us. For I am convinced that neither death nor life, neither angels nor demons, neither the present nor the future, nor any powers, neither height nor depth, nor anything else in all creation, will be able to separate us from the love of God that is in Christ Jesus our Lord.

Devotional

Most of us place a higher premium on what other people think than we realize. As can be seen in Galatians, the apostle Paul understood this struggle intimately.

M. Scott Peck illustrates the point through a story of meeting a high school classmate at the age of fifteen. Here are his reflections after a conversation with his friend:

I suddenly realized that for the entire ten-minute period from when I had first seen my acquaintance until that very moment, I had been totally self-preoccupied. For the two or three minutes before we met, all I was thinking about was the clever things I might say that would impress him. During our five minutes together, I was listening to what he had to say only so that I might turn it into a clever rejoinder. I watched him only so that I might see what effect my remarks were having upon him. And for the two or three minutes after we separated, my sole thought was of those things I could have said that might have impressed him even more.

I had not cared a whit for my classmate.[23]

What is most startling in reading this detailed explanation of what was going on beneath the surface of this fifteen-year-old boy, is the recognition that the same dynamics continue for most of us into our twenties, thirties, fifties, seventies, and nineties! We remain trapped in living a pretend life — always seeking the approval of others.

True freedom comes when we no longer need to be special in other people's eyes because we know we are loveable and good enough in Christ.

Question to Consider

How might it change your day today if you were to cease looking for human approval and begin seeking only the approval of God?

Prayer

Grant me courage, Lord, to do today what you have given me to do, to say what you have given me to say, and to become who you have called me to become. In Jesus' name, amen.

Conclude with Silence (2 minutes)

DAY 5: MIDDAY/EVENING OFFICE

Silence, Stillness, and Centering before God (2 minutes)

Scripture Reading: Isaiah 40:28 – 31

Do you not know?
    Have you not heard?

51

The LORD is the everlasting God,
    the Creator of the ends of the earth.
He will not grow tired or weary,
    and his understanding no one can fathom.
He gives strength to the weary
    and increases the power of the weak.
Even youths grow tired and weary,
    and young men stumble and fall;
but those who hope in the LORD
    will renew their strength.
They will soar on wings like eagles;
    they will run and not grow weary,
    they will walk and not be faint.

Devotional

In his book *The Song of the Bird*, Tony de Mello tells the following story:

> A man found an eagle's egg and put it in a nest of a barnyard hen. The eaglet hatched with the brood of chicks and grew up with them.
>
> All his life the eagle did what the barnyard chicks did, thinking he was a barnyard chick. He scratched the earth for worms and insects, he clucked and cackled. And he would thrash his wings and fly a few feet into the air.
>
> Years passed and the eagle grew very old. One day he saw a magnificent bird above him in the cloudless sky. It glided in graceful majesty among the powerful wind currents, with scarcely a beat of its strong golden wings. The eagle looked up in awe. "Who's that?" he asked.
>
> "That's the eagle, the king of the birds," said his neighbor. "He belongs to the sky. We belong to the earth — we are chickens."

So the eagle lived and died a chicken, for that's what he thought he was.[24]

Question to Consider

In what area of your life might you be living as a chicken when God, in reality, has made you an eagle?

Prayer

Father, you have made me a golden eagle — able to fly. In so many ways, however, I still live as a chicken, unaware of the heights and the richness to which you have called me. Fill me, Holy Spirit. Set me free to be the unique person the Lord Jesus has created me to be. In Jesus' name, amen.

Conclude with Silence (2 minutes)

Going Back
in Order to Go Forward

DAY 1: MORNING/MIDDAY OFFICE

Silence, Stillness, and Centering before God (2 minutes)

Scripture Reading: Hebrews 11:24–27

> By faith Moses, when he had grown up, refused to be known as the son of Pharaoh's daughter. He chose to be mistreated along with the people of God rather than to enjoy the fleeting pleasures of sin. He regarded disgrace for the sake of Christ as of greater value than the treasures of Egypt, because he was looking ahead to his reward. By faith he left Egypt, not fearing the king's anger; he persevered because he saw him who is invisible.

Devotional

Even the worst and most painful family experiences become part of our total identity. God had a plan in placing us in our particular families and cultures. And the more we know about our families, the more we know about ourselves — and the more freedom we have to make decisions about how we want to live.

If we ignore the truth out of fear, we will end up like Miss Havisham from Charles Dickens's novel *Great Expectations*. The daughter of a wealthy man, she received a letter at 8:40 a.m. on her wedding day, saying that her husband-to-be was not coming. She stopped all clocks in the house at the precise time the letter arrived and spent the rest of her life in her bridal dress (which eventually turned yellow), and wearing only one shoe (since she had not yet put on the other one at the time of the disaster). Even as an old lady she remained crippled by the weight of that crushing blow. It was as if "everything in the room and house had stopped." She decided to live in her past, not her present or future.[25]

Moses' life had more than its share of pain and failure. After being raised in a wealthy, privileged home, he murdered a man, lost everything, and spent the next forty years of his life in obscurity in the desert. Yet, by faith he "sees him who is invisible" and hears God's invitation to do something that will be a blessing to many.

Question to Consider

What invitation might God be offering to you out of the failures and pain of your past?

Prayer

Lord Jesus, set me free to be the person you have destined me to be. Help me to pause to hear your voice today, and to leave behind the "baggage" I am carrying as I seek to follow you. Help me to discern your hand at work in and through my life, both in the past and the future. In Jesus' name, amen.

Conclude with Silence (2 minutes)

DAY 1: MIDDAY/EVENING OFFICE

Silence, Stillness, and Centering before God (2 minutes)

Scripture Reading: Luke 9:59 – 62

[Jesus] said to another man, "Follow me."

But he replied, "Lord, first let me go and bury my father."

Jesus said to him, "Let the dead bury their own dead, but you go and proclaim the kingdom of God."

Still another said, "I will follow you, Lord; but first let me go back and say goodbye to my family."

Jesus replied, "No one who puts a hand to the plow and looks back is fit for service in the kingdom of God."

Devotional

There's an old story about a boy who, having grown up at the edge of a wide, turbulent river, spent his childhood learning to build rafts. When the boy reached manhood, he felled some trees, lashed them together, and riding his raft, he crossed to the far side of the river. Because he had spent so long working on the raft, he couldn't see leaving it behind when he reached dry land, so he lashed it to his shoulders and carried it with him, though all he came upon in his journeys were a few easily fordable streams and puddles. He rarely thought about the things he was missing out on because he was carrying the bulky raft — the trees he couldn't climb, vistas he couldn't see, people he couldn't get close to and races he couldn't run. He didn't even realize how heavy the raft was, because he had never known what it was like to be free of it.

— Lori Gordon[26]

While all of us are affected by powerful external events and circumstances throughout our earthly lives, our families of origin are the most influential group to which we will ever belong. Even those who leave home as young adults, determined to "break" from their family history, soon find their family's way of "doing life" follows them wherever they go.

Family patterns from the past are played out in our present relationships — often without us necessarily being aware of it. The price we pay for this is high. Our family history lives inside of all of us, even in those who attempt to bury it.

Only the truth sets us free. What was learned can be unlearned. And by God's grace and power, we can learn new ways of "doing life," making change and freedom possible.

Question to Consider

What heavy "raft" might you be carrying as you seek to climb the mountains God has placed before you?

Prayer

Lord, I too prefer to not look at or remember the painful past. Show me, O Father, the heavy weights and rafts I am carrying due to my past. Help me to learn what it means to honestly face my past, lift it up to you, and allow you to use it as a means to my maturing and growing in Christ. In Jesus' name, amen.

Conclude with Silence (2 minutes)

DAY 2: MORNING/MIDDAY OFFICE

Silence, Stillness, and Centering before God (2 minutes)

Scripture Reading: Mark 3:31 – 35

Then Jesus' mother and brothers arrived. Standing outside, they sent someone in to call him. A crowd was sitting around him, and they told him, "Your mother and brothers are outside looking for you."

"Who are my mother and my brothers?" he asked.

Then he looked at those seated in a circle around him and said, "Here are my mother and my brothers! Whoever does God's will is my brother and sister and mother."

Devotional

When we become Christians we are adopted into the family of Jesus. Jesus was clear and direct in calling people to have a first loyalty to him. Discipleship, he made clear, is putting off the sinful patterns of unbelief so that we might put on the choices of faith, being transformed to live as members of Jesus' family.

As we go back to go forward, we find that it is a never-ending process. We go back, breaking some destructive power of the past. Then later, on a deeper level, God has us return to the same issue on a more profound level.

Thomas Keating compares God's work in us to a Middle Eastern "tell," or archeological site, where one civilization is built on another in the same place. Archeologists excavate, level by level, culture by culture, down through history. The Holy Spirit, he says, is like a Divine Archeologist digging through the layers of our lives.

> The Spirit intends to investigate our whole life history, layer by layer, throwing out the junk and preserving the values that were appropriate to each stage of our human development.... Eventually, the Spirit begins to dig into the bedrock of our earliest emotional life.... Hence, as we progress toward the center where God actually is waiting for us, we are naturally going to feel that we are getting worse. This warns us that the spiritual journey is not a success story or a career move. It is rather a series of humiliations of the false self.[27]

Question to Consider

What false self are you struggling with that Christ wants you to die to so that you can truly live?

Prayer

Holy Spirit, I invite you to dig through the layers of my being that hinder my relationships and communion with others. Grant me perseverance to allow you to dig deeply, excavating out of me all that is not of Christ so that I may be filled with your presence. In Jesus' name, amen.

Conclude with Silence (2 minutes)

DAY 2: MIDDAY/EVENING OFFICE

Silence, Stillness, and Centering before God (2 minutes)

Scripture Reading: Hebrews 12:1 – 3

Therefore, since we are surrounded by such a great cloud of witnesses, let us throw off everything that hinders and the sin that so easily entangles. And let us run with perseverance the race marked out for us, fixing our eyes on Jesus, the pioneer and perfecter of faith. For the joy set before him he endured the cross, scorning its shame, and sat down at the right hand of the throne of God. Consider him who endured such opposition from sinners, so that you will not grow weary and lose heart.

Devotional

Francis of Assisi, one of the most influential Christians in the past two thousand years, broke with his family in a very dramatic way. As Francis grew more passionate about his relationship with Christ and less interested in his father's lucrative business, their tension grew. This climaxed in the following scene:

The father [dragged] the son before the local bishop in the hopes that the town's religious authority could talk some sense into the young man. But the plan backfired. There in front of God and everybody, Francis stripped off his clothing and handed it to his father. Standing there naked as the day he was born, Francis said, "Until now I called you father, but from now on I can say without reserve, 'Our father who art in heaven.'"

Francis's father carried his son's clothes back to a large house that was now strangely quiet. Francis, on the other hand, went on his way rejoicing, suddenly freed from the encumbrances of wealth, family, and social esteem....

But one final barrier was left to cross before he could serve God with his whole heart. One day as he was walking down the road and saw a leper approaching him, he knew his opportunity was at hand.... Francis reached out and kissed him.[28]

Francis of Assisi represents one of the "great cloud of witnesses" mentioned in Hebrews 12. He literally "threw off everything that hindered him" and was launched by God into an extraordinary life and destiny. His life continues to speak to us today.

Questions to Consider

What most impacts you in this story about Francis? How is God speaking to you through it?

Prayer

Lord, there is none like you. I want to know you as my ultimate Father, the one whose unfathomable, unconditional love sets me free to live for you — far above all other loyalties and expectations. In Jesus' name, amen.

Conclude with Silence (2 minutes)

DAY 3: MORNING/MIDDAY OFFICE

Silence, Stillness, and Centering before God (2 minutes)

Scripture Reading: Genesis 50:15, 19 – 21

When Joseph's brothers saw that their father was dead, they said, "What if Joseph holds a grudge against us and pays us back for all the wrongs we did to him?"

His brothers then came and threw themselves down before him. "We are your slaves," they said.

But Joseph said to them, "Don't be afraid. Am I in the place of God? You intended to harm me, but God intended it for good to accomplish what is now being done, the saving of many lives. So then, don't be afraid. I will provide for you and your children." And he reassured them and spoke kindly to them.

Devotional

Joseph was born into a family characterized by great brokenness and sadness. Lying, jealousy, secrecy, and betrayal visited upon Joseph's young life, and he spent ten to thirteen years in prison, completely cut off from his family.

Nonetheless, Joseph was able to observe the large, loving hand of God through all his setbacks and disappointments. In doing so, he affirmed that God mysteriously leads us into his purposes through darkness and obscurity. God is the Lord God Almighty who has all history in his grip, working in ways that are mostly hidden to us on earth. Joseph understood that in all things God is at work — in spite of, through, and against all human effort — orchestrating his purposes.[29]

God never discards any of our past for his future when we surrender ourselves to him. He is the Lord! Every mistake, sin, and detour we take in the journey of life is taken by God and becomes his gift for a future of blessing when we surrender ourselves to him.

Why did God allow Joseph to go through such pain and loss?

We see traces of the good that came out of it in Genesis 37 – 50, but much remains a mystery. Most important for us to recognize today is that Joseph did not deny his past but trusted in God's goodness and love, even when circumstances went from bad to worse.[30]

Question to Consider

What would it look like for you to surrender the pains of your past (mistakes, sins, setbacks, and disappointments) to God today?

Prayer

Father, I affirm with Joseph that you sovereignly placed me into my family, my culture, and my present circumstances. I cannot see all that you see, but I ask you to show me how, like Joseph, I can rest in your love and power — even when I can't see any good that you might be doing. In Jesus' name, amen.

Conclude with Silence (2 minutes)

DAY 3: MIDDAY/EVENING OFFICE

Silence, Stillness, and Centering before God (2 minutes)

Scripture Reading: Genesis 45:4 – 7

Then Joseph said to his brothers, "Come close to me." When they had done so, he said, "I am your brother Joseph, the one you sold into Egypt! And now, do not be distressed and do not be angry with yourselves for selling me here, because it was to save lives that God sent me ahead of you. For two years now there has been famine in the land, and for the next five years there will not be plowing and reaping. But God sent me ahead of you to preserve for you a remnant on earth and to save your lives by a great deliverance."

Devotional

Most of us resist remembering and feeling the hurt and pain of our past. It can feel like an abyss that might swallow us up. We can wonder if we are only getting worse. Yet Joseph wept repeatedly when he reunited with his family. In fact, Scripture relates that he wept so loudly that the Egyptians heard him (Genesis 45:2).

Joseph did not minimize or rationalize the painful years of his life. He could have destroyed his brothers in anger. Instead, out of the honest grieving of his pain, he genuinely forgave the brothers who had betrayed him, and was able to bless them. Joseph was able to discern that God had sent him ahead to Egypt to save his brothers' lives by a great deliverance (Genesis 45:7).

The question is, "How did he do it?"

Joseph clearly developed a secret history over a long period of time in his relationship with God. His whole life was structured around following the Lord God of Israel. Then, when the moment came for him to make a critical decision, he was ready. He took leadership of his family — and continued to the end of his days — providing for them financially, emotionally, and spiritually.

Question to Consider

What pains in your life are waiting to be acknowledged and grieved?

Prayer

> *Lord, lead me through the process of grieving and healing that I might offer genuine kindness and forgiveness to those who have not been kind to me. Help me, like Joseph, to join with you to become a blessing to many other people. In Jesus' name, amen.*

Conclude with Silence (2 minutes)

DAY 4: MORNING/MIDDAY OFFICE

Silence, Stillness, and Centering before God (2 minutes)

Scripture Reading: Acts 9:1 – 6, 15 – 16

Meanwhile, Saul was still breathing out murderous threats against the Lord's disciples. He went to the high priest and asked him for letters to the synagogues in Damascus, so that if he found any there who belonged to the Way, whether men or women, he might take them as prisoners to Jerusalem. As he neared Damascus on his journey, suddenly a light from heaven flashed around him. He fell to the ground and heard a voice say to him, "Saul, Saul, why do you persecute me?"

"Who are you, Lord?" Saul asked.

"I am Jesus, whom you are persecuting," he replied. "Now get up and go into the city, and you will be told what you must do."

But the Lord said to Ananias, "Go! This man is my chosen instrument to proclaim my name to the Gentiles and their kings and to the people of Israel. I will show him how much he must suffer for my name."

Devotional

Saul's great conversion and life as an apostle can only be understood by looking at his entire life and training leading up to this famous passage in Acts 9.

Søren Kierkegaard once observed that life is lived forward, but only understood backward. This was certainly Aleksandr Solzhenitsyn's experience.

Solzhenitsyn is considered by many to be the greatest Russian writer of the twentieth century, but his sense of calling was not always clear. His purpose grew in his experiences of the Gulag, the Soviet concentration camps — a place where he experienced a deadly struggle to write, a miracle of a cure from cancer, a conversion through a Jewish follower of Jesus, and a deepening burden to put "the dying wish of millions" on record. He wrote:

> The one worrying thing was that I might not be given time to carry out the whole scheme. I felt as though I was about to fill a space in the world that was meant for me and had long awaited me, a mold, as it were, made for me alone, but discerned by me only this very moment. I was a molten substance, impatient, unendurably impatient, to pour into my mold, to fill it full, without air bubbles or cracks, before I cooled and stiffened....
>
> Later, the true significance of what happened would inevitably become clear to me, and I would be numb with surprise.[31]

Question to Consider
What space in the world (for which your past has prepared you) is waiting to be filled by you?

Prayer
Lord, you are good, and your love endures forever. Help me to trust you — with the good as well as the difficult, the successes and the failures, the joys and the sorrows of my past. I surrender to your voice that whispers to me, "All is well, and all will be well." In Jesus' name, amen.

Conclude with Silence (2 minutes)

DAY 4: MIDDAY/EVENING OFFICE

Silence, Stillness, and Centering before God (2 minutes)

Scripture Reading: 1 Samuel 16:6 – 7

> When they arrived, Samuel saw Eliab and thought, "Surely the Lord's anointed stands here before the LORD."
>
> But the LORD said to Samuel, "Do not consider his appearance or his height, for I have rejected him. The LORD does not look at the things people look at. People look at the outward appearance, but the LORD looks at the heart."

Devotional

Chaim Potok, in his novel *The Chosen*, tells the story of a friendship between two boys growing up in Brooklyn, New York. Danny is a strict Hasidic Jew, and Reuven is a conservative Jew. Danny's father is the leader of a Hasidic community and raises his son in silence. He never speaks to him directly.

Danny is hurt and confused. He cannot understand why his father is so distant and afflicts him with so much pain. At the end of the novel, Danny's father explains that he did it for him as an act of love.

Danny later reflects on the painful experience: "My father never talked to me, except when we studied together. He taught me with silence. He taught me to look into myself, to find my own strength, to walk inside myself in company with my soul."

In the book, Danny discovers that the suffering he experienced had a good outcome. "One learns of the pain of others by suffering one's own pain, by turning inside oneself, by finding one's own soul. And it is important to know of pain. It destroys our self-pride, our arrogance, and our indifference toward others. It makes us aware of how frail and tiny we are and of how much we must depend upon the Master of the Universe."[32]

In reading 1 Samuel 16, one has to wonder what life was like for David as the youngest of seven sons. What did he learn from being considered invisible, not only by his brothers, but his father as well? How might this experience have helped to shape his character so that he is later called "a man after God's own heart"?

Question to Consider

Can you name some of the ways in which you have learned the pain of others by suffering your own pain?

Prayer

Father, may the pains I experience in life kill the things that need to die in me — arrogance, pride, and indifference to others. Help me, daily, to see my frailty and how dependent I am on you, the Master of the Universe. In Jesus' name, amen.

Conclude with Silence (2 minutes)

DAY 5: MORNING/MIDDAY OFFICE

Silence, Stillness, and Centering before God (2 minutes)

Scripture Reading: Exodus 14:10, 13 – 16

As Pharaoh approached, the Israelites looked up, and there were the Egyptians, marching after them. They were terrified and cried out to the LORD.

Moses answered the people, "Do not be afraid. Stand firm and you will see the deliverance the LORD will bring you today. The Egyptians you see today you will never see again.

The LORD will fight for you; you need only to be still."

Then the LORD said to Moses, "Why are you crying out to me? Tell the Israelites to move on. Raise your staff and stretch out your hand over the sea to divide the water so that the Israelites can go through the sea on dry ground."

Devotional

Moses demonstrated godly leadership as Egypt's army was overtaking the Israelites at the Red Sea. However, in their anxiety, the Israelites distorted the past and refused to move forward. They preferred their miserable past to an unknown future with God.

Moses courageously stands alone and calls them to "be still" and to "move on." He picks up his staff and takes deliberate steps to move ahead. By remembering the Lord (being still), Moses courageously does what is best (moving on), despite the Israelites' lack of support. He models the delicate balance of being still while at the same time moving on. In doing so, he transforms not only his own life, but the life of all those around him.

Everyone who draws breath "takes the lead" many times a day. We lead with actions that range from a smile to a frown; with words that range from blessing to curse; with decisions that range from faithful to fearful.... When I resist thinking of myself as a leader, it is neither because of modesty nor a clear-eyed look at the reality of my life.... I am responsible for my impact on the world whether I acknowledge it or not.

So, what does it take to qualify as a leader? Being human and being here. As long as I am here, doing whatever I am doing, I am leading, for better or for worse. And, if I may say so, so are you.

— Parker Palmer[33]

Question to Consider

How might the words from Exodus 14:14 – 15 — "The Lord will fight for you, you need only to be still" and "move on" — apply to you today?

Prayer

Lord, I can relate to the Israelites in the desert and their desire to return to what is predictable — even if it is miserable. Change is hard. Grant me the courage of Moses to walk the delicate balance of being still and moving on to the new life in Christ that you have for me. In Jesus' name, amen.

Conclude with Silence (2 minutes)

DAY 5: MIDDAY/EVENING OFFICE

Silence, Stillness, and Centering before God (2 minutes)

Scripture Reading: Psalm 131

My heart is not proud, Lord,
    my eyes are not haughty;
I do not concern myself with great matters
    or things too wonderful for me.
But I have calmed and quieted myself,
    I am like a weaned child with its mother;
    like a weaned child I am content.
Israel, put your hope in the Lord
    both now and forevermore.

Devotional

We often forget our humanity, our limits, and our inability to change others. Considering that David was one of the more powerful people in his day, it is striking how he reminds himself in this psalm to not think too highly of himself.

The following quotation is from an anonymous Hasidic rabbi on his deathbed. These words have served me well over the years; they keep me focused on Christ changing me:

> When I was young, I set out to change the world. When I grew a little older, I perceived that this was too ambitious, so I set out to change my state. This too, I realized as I grew older, was too ambitious, so I set out to change my town. When I realized I could not even do this, I tried to change my family. Now as an old man, I know that I should have started by changing myself. If I had started with myself, maybe then I would have succeeded in changing my family, the town, or even the state — and who knows, maybe even the world![34]

Question to Consider

In Psalm 131:1 David prays: "I do not concern myself with great matters or things too wonderful for me." How do you hear these words?

Prayer

Lord Jesus, give my heart eyes to see and ears to hear the ways I need to change. May I be more deeply, radically, and powerfully transformed for your name's sake. Amen.

Conclude with Silence (2 minutes)

Journey through the Wall

DAY 1: MORNING/MIDDAY OFFICE

Silence, Stillness, and Centering before God (2 minutes)

Scripture Reading: Genesis 12:1 – 3

The LORD had said to Abram, "Go from your country, your people and your father's household to the land I will show you.

"I will make you into a great nation,
 and I will bless you;
I will make your name great,
 and you will be a blessing.
I will bless those who bless you,
 and whoever curses you I will curse;
and all peoples on earth
 will be blessed through you."

Devotional

Like few other metaphors, the image of the Christian life as a journey captures our experience of following Christ. Journeys involve movement, action, stops and starts, detours, delays, and trips into the unknown.

God called Abraham to leave his comfortable life in Ur at the age of seventy-five and to embark on a long, slow journey — a journey with God that would require much patient trust.

Patient Trust

Above all, trust in the slow work of God. We are quite naturally impatient in everything to reach the end without delay. We should like to skip the intermediate stages. We are impatient of being on the way to something unknown, something new. And yet it is the law of all progress that it is made by passing through some stages of instability — and that it may take a very long time.

And so I think it is with you; your ideas mature gradually — let them grow, let them shape themselves, without undue haste. Don't try to force them on, as though you could be today what time (that is to say, grace and circumstances acting on your own good will) will make of you tomorrow.

Only God could say what this new spirit gradually forming within you will be. Give our Lord the benefit of believing that his hand is leading you. And accept the anxiety of feeling yourself in suspense and incomplete.

— Pierre Teilhard de Chardin[35]

Question to Consider

What does it mean for you to trust in the slow work of God today?

Prayer

Grant me courage, Father, to embark on the unique journey you have crafted for me. By faith, I surrender my need and desire to be in control of every event, circumstance, and person I will meet today. In Jesus' name, amen.

Conclude with Silence (2 minutes)

DAY 1: MIDDAY/EVENING OFFICE

Silence, Stillness, and Centering before God (2 minutes)

Scripture Reading: Song of Songs 1:2, 3:1 – 3

Let him kiss me with the kisses of his mouth —
for your love is more delightful than wine....

All night long on my bed
    I looked for the one my heart loves;
    I looked for him but did not find him.
I will get up now and go about the city,
    through its streets and squares;
I will search for the one my heart loves.
    So I looked for him but did not find him.
The watchmen found me
    as they made their rounds in the city.
    "Have you seen the one my heart loves?"

Devotional

Christians primarily read the Song of Songs on two levels: as the marital love of a man and woman, and as a description of our love relationship with the Lord Jesus — our Bridegroom. Song of Songs 3:1 – 3 describes, in particular, the experience of Mother Teresa of Calcutta. Regarding her painful struggle with God's absence throughout her fifty-year service among the poor, she wrote:

> When I try to raise my thoughts to Heaven — there is such convicting emptiness that those very thoughts return like sharp knives and hurt my very soul. Love — the word — it brings nothing. I am told God loves me — and yet the reality of darkness and coldness and emptiness is so great that nothing touches my soul....
>
> In spite of all — this darkness and emptiness is not as painful as the longing for God....
>
> Before I could spend hours before Our Lord — loving Him — talking to Him — and now — not even meditation goes properly.... Yet deep down somewhere in my heart that longing for God keeps breaking through the darkness....
>
> My soul is just like [an] ice block — I have nothing to say.[36]

Mother Teresa came to realize that her darkness was the spiritual side of her work, a sharing in Christ's suffering, a treasure for her and her unique work. She eventually wrote: "I have come to love the darkness. For I believe that it is a part, a very small part, of Jesus' darkness and pain on earth."[37]

Question to Consider

What treasures might there be in the darkness or difficulties in your own life today?

Prayer

Father, teach me to trust you even when I feel like I am alone and that you are asleep in the boat with storms raging all around me. Awaken me to the treasures that can only be found in darkness. Grant me the grace to follow you into the next place you have for me in this journey called life. In Jesus' name, amen.

Conclude with Silence (2 minutes)

DAY 2: MORNING/MIDDAY OFFICE

Silence, Stillness, and Centering before God (2 minutes)

Scripture Reading: Hebrews 12:7 – 11

Endure hardship as discipline; God is treating you as his children. For what children are not disciplined by their father? If you are not disciplined — and everyone undergoes discipline — then you are not legitimate, not true sons and daughters at all. Moreover, we have all had human fathers who disciplined us and we respected them for it. How much more should we submit to the Father of our spirits and live! They disciplined us for a little while as they thought best; but God disciplines us for our good, in order that we may share in his holiness. No discipline seems pleasant at the time, but painful. Later on, however, it produces a harvest of righteousness and peace for those who have been trained by it.

Devotional

The best way to understand the dynamics of suffering is to examine the classic work of St. John of the Cross entitled *Dark Night of the Soul*, written over five hundred years ago. St. John describes the spiritual journey in three phases: beginners, progressives, and perfect. To move out of the beginning stage, he argues, requires receiving God's gift of the dark night, or the wall. This is the ordinary way we grow in Christ.

The wall is God's way of rewiring and "purging our affections and passions" so that we might delight in his love and enter into a richer, fuller communion with him. God works to free us from unhealthy worldly attachments and idolatries. He wants to communicate his true sweetness and love to us. He longs for us to know his true peace and rest.

For this reason, John of the Cross wrote that God sends us "the dark night of loving fire" to free us from such deadly spiritual imperfections as pride (being judgmental and impatient with the faults of others), avarice (suffering discontentment), luxury (taking more pleasure in our spiritual blessings than in God himself), wrath (becoming easily irritated or impatient), spiritual gluttony (resisting the cross), spiritual envy (always comparing ourselves to others), and sloth (running from what is hard).[38]

Question to Consider

What are some unhealthy attachments or idols God wants to remove from your life in order to lead you to a deeper, richer communion with him?

Prayer

Lord, I invite you this day to cut any unhealthy attachments or idols out of me. You promise in Psalm 32 to teach me the way to go. Help me not to be stubborn like a mule, but rather to be cooperative as you seek to lead me to freedom. Lead me to a place of communion with you, where true peace and rest is found. In Jesus' name, amen.

Conclude with Silence (2 minutes)

DAY 2: MIDDAY/EVENING OFFICE

Silence, Stillness, and Centering before God (2 minutes)

Scripture Reading: Genesis 22:9 – 12

When they reached the place God had told him about, Abraham built an altar there and arranged the wood on it. He bound his son Isaac and laid him on the altar, on top of the wood. Then he reached out his hand and took the knife to slay his son. But the angel of the LORD called out to him from heaven, "Abraham! Abraham!"

"Here I am," he replied.

"Do not lay a hand on the boy," he said. "Do not do anything to him. Now I know that you fear God, because you have not withheld from me your son, your only son."

Devotional

We encounter the wall when a crisis turns our world upside down. These walls are not simply one-time events that we pass through and get beyond. They are issues we return to as a part of our ongoing relationship with God.

We see this in Abraham, waiting at the wall of infertility for twenty-five years before the birth of his first child with his wife, Sarah. Ten to thirteen years later, God led him to another wall — the separation from Ishmael, his eldest son (conceived with Sarah's maidservant, Hagar). Abraham encountered a third wall a few years later, when God commanded him to sacrifice his long-awaited, beloved son Isaac on the altar.

Abraham appears to have gone through the wall numerous times in his journey with God. Why? Thomas Merton explains, "Unintentionally and unknowingly we fall back into imperfections. Bad habits are like living roots that return. These roots must be dug away and cleared from the garden of our soul.... This requires the direct intervention of God."[39]

Question to Consider

What things or people are you rooting your identity in that God may want to dig up so that your identity might be replanted in him?

Prayer

Abba Father, I open my clenched fists to surrender everything you have given to me. Reestablish my identity in you — not in my family, my work, my accomplishments, or what others think of me. Cleanse the things in me that are not conformed to your will. By faith I unite my will to yours so that the likeness of Jesus Christ may be formed in me. In his name, amen.

Conclude with Silence (2 minutes)

DAY 3: MORNING/MIDDAY OFFICE

Silence, Stillness, and Centering before God (2 minutes)

Scripture Reading: Romans 11:33–36

> Oh, the depth of the riches of the wisdom and knowledge of God!
>> How unsearchable his judgments,
>> and his paths beyond tracing out!
> "Who has known the mind of the Lord?
>> Or who has been his counselor?"
> "Who has ever given to God,
>> that God should repay them?"
> For from him and through him and for him are all things.
>> To him be the glory forever! Amen.

Devotional

Our experience at the wall can be fruitful in providing a greater appreciation for what I call "holy unknowing" or mystery. This expands our capacity to wait on God when everything inside us is saying, "Do something!"

There is an old story about a wise man living on one of China's vast frontiers. One day, for no apparent reason, a young man's horse ran away and was taken by nomads across the border. Everyone tried to offer consolation for the man's bad fortune, but his father, a wise man, said, "What makes you so sure this is not a blessing?"

Months later, his horse returned, bringing with her a magnificent stallion. This time everyone was full of congratulations for the son's good fortune. But now his father said, "What makes you so sure this isn't a disaster?"

Their household was made richer by this fine horse the son loved to ride, but one day he fell off his horse and broke his hip.

Once again, everyone offered their consolation for his bad luck, but his father said, "What makes you so sure this is not a blessing?"

A year later, nomads invaded, and every able-bodied man was required to take up his bow and go into battle. The Chinese families living on the border lost nine out of every ten men who went to fight. Only because the son was lame did the father and son survive to take care of each other.

Often, what appears to be success or a blessing is actually a terrible thing; what appears to be a terrible event can turn out to be a rich blessing.[40]

Question to Consider

Have you ever experienced a terrible circumstance that (in time) actually turned out to be a rich blessing?

Prayer

Forgive me, Father, for at times treating you as if you were my personal assistant or secretary. Your ways are unsearchable and beyond understanding. Help me to put my trust in you and not in my circumstances. In your presence, I am silenced. In Jesus' name, amen.

Conclude with Silence (2 minutes)

DAY 3: MIDDAY/EVENING OFFICE

Silence, Stillness, and Centering before God (2 minutes)

Scripture Reading: Job 42:1 – 6

Then Job replied to the LORD:

"I know that you can do all things;
    no plan of yours can be thwarted.

You asked, 'Who is this that obscures my counsel without
knowledge?'
> Surely I spoke of things I did not understand,
> things too wonderful for me to know.
You said, 'Listen now, and I will speak;
> I will question you,
> and you shall answer me.'
My ears had heard of you
> but now my eyes have seen you.
Therefore I despise myself
> and repent in dust and ashes." (NIV 1984)

Devotional

Job was faithful and blameless, a man of integrity. Yet he experienced the cataclysmic loss of his family, wealth, and health, and
found himself at a wall like few others in all of Scripture. From this
place of deep wrestling with his faith and God, he experiences God's
love and grace. He is transformed.

> Now, believe it or not, we are threatened by such a free God be-
> cause it takes away all of our ability to control or engineer the
> process. It leaves us powerless, and changes the language from
> any language of performance or achievement to that of surren-
> der, trust and vulnerability.... That is the so-called "wildness"
> of God. We cannot control God by any means whatsoever,
> not even by our good behavior, which tends to be our first and
> natural instinct.... That utter and absolute freedom of God is
> fortunately used totally in our favor, even though we are still
> afraid of it. It is called providence, forgiveness, free election or
> mercy.... But to us, it feels like wildness — precisely because

we cannot control it, manipulate it, direct it, earn it or lose it. Anyone into controlling God by his or her actions will feel very useless, impotent and ineffective.

— Richard Rohr[41]

Questions to Consider

What words or phrases from the Richard Rohr quote most speak to you? Why?

Prayer

Father, when I read even part of the story of Job, I too am overwhelmed by your "wildness." Your ways and timing are beyond me. Job moved from hearing about you to having "seen you." Lead me, Lord, on a pathway so that I too can pray as Job prayed: "My ears had heard of you, but now my eyes have seen you" (Job 42:5). In Jesus' name, amen.

Conclude with Silence (2 minutes)

DAY 4: MORNING/MIDDAY OFFICE

Silence, Stillness, and Centering before God (2 minutes)

Scripture Reading: Psalm 69:1 – 3, 15 – 16

Save me, O God,
    for the waters have come up to my neck.
I sink in the miry depths,
    where there is no foothold.
I have come into the deep waters;
    the floods engulf me.
I am worn out calling for help;
    my throat is parched.

My eyes fail,
>> looking for my God.
Do not let the floodwaters engulf me
>> or the depths swallow me up
>> or the pit close its mouth over me.
Answer me, LORD, out of the goodness of your love;
>> in your great mercy turn to me.

Devotional

The Bible presents David as a man after God's own heart, yet the preceding Scripture reading shows us that David's emotional world was very human and broken. He bares his soul in these heart-wrenching poems — as prayers back to God. While he often struggles with his circumstances, David affirms that God is good, and that his love endures forever. David knows that God's ways are higher and deeper than our ways (Isaiah 55:9 – 10).

In *Paradise Lost*, John Milton compares the evil of history to a compost pile — a mixture of decaying substances such as animal excrement, potato skins, egg shells, dead leaves, and banana peels. If you cover it with dirt, after some time it smells wonderful. The soil has become a rich, natural fertilizer and is tremendously well suited for growing fruits and vegetables — but you have to be willing to wait — years, in some cases.

Milton's point is that the worst events of human history — those that we cannot understand — even hell itself — are compost in God's wonderful eternal plan. Out of the greatest evil, the death of Jesus, came the greatest good.

The fact that God exists does not lessen the awfulness of the evil in the world; nevertheless, we can rest in him, placing our hope in a God who is so great and sovereign that he ultimately transforms all evil into good.[42]

We can trust God at the Wall.

Question to Consider

How is God inviting you to wait on him today?

Prayer

Lord, fill me with the simple trust that even out of the most awful evil around me, you are able to bring great good — for me, for others, and for your great glory. In Jesus' name, amen.

Conclude with Silence (2 minutes)

DAY 4: MIDDAY/EVENING OFFICE

Silence, Stillness, and Centering before God (2 minutes)

Scripture Reading: John 21:17 – 19

The third time he said to him, "Simon son of John, do you love me?"

Peter was hurt because Jesus asked him the third time, "Do you love me?" He said, "Lord, you know all things; you know that I love you."

Jesus said, "Feed my sheep. Very truly I tell you, when you were younger you dressed yourself and went where you wanted; but when you are old you will stretch out your hands, and someone else will dress you and lead you where you do not want to go." Jesus said this to indicate the kind of death by which Peter would glorify God. Then he said to him, "Follow me!"

Devotional

Jesus had this different vision of maturity: It is the ability and willingness to be led where you would rather not go. Immediately after Jesus commissions Peter to be a leader of his sheep, Jesus confronts Peter with the hard truth that the servant-leader is the leader who is being led to unknown, undesirable, and painful places. Henri Nouwen expressed it well:

> The way of the Christian leader is not the way of upward mobility in which our world has invested so much, but the way of downward mobility ending on the cross.... Powerlessness and humility in the spiritual life do not refer to people who have no spine and who let everyone make decisions for them. They refer to people who are so deeply in love with Jesus that they are ready to follow him wherever he guides them, always trusting that, with him, they will find life and find it abundantly.[43]

Question to Consider

In your own words, speak to God about your willingness to go where he leads you. What joys and/or fears accompany your willingness?

Prayer

Father, to you I acknowledge that I don't want to go the way of powerlessness and humility. Like Peter, I want to know what you are doing with those around me. I love you. Help me to trust you with this day, with tomorrow, and with my whole life. In Jesus' name, amen.

Conclude with Silence (2 minutes)

DAY 5: MORNING/MIDDAY OFFICE

Silence, Stillness, and Centering before God (2 minutes)

Scripture Reading: James 1:2 – 5

Consider it pure joy, my brothers and sisters, whenever you face trials of many kinds, because you know that the testing of your faith produces perseverance. Let perseverance finish its work so that you may be mature and complete, not lacking anything. If any of you lacks wisdom, you should ask God, who gives generously to all without finding fault, and it will be given to you.

Devotional

If there were never any storms or clouds in our lives, we would have no faith. "His way is in the whirlwind and the storm, and clouds are the dust of his feet" (Nahum 1:3b). Clouds are a sign that God is there. What a revelation to know that sorrow, bereavement, and suffering are actually the clouds that come along with God!

It is not true to say that God wants to teach us something in our trials. Through every cloud He brings our way, He wants us to unlearn something. His purpose in using the cloud is to simplify our beliefs until our relationship with Him is exactly like that of a child — a relationship simply between God and our own souls, and where other people are but shadows. Until other people become shadows to us, clouds and darkness will be ours every once in a while. Is our relationship with God becoming more simple than it has ever been?… Until we come face to face with the deepest, darkest fact of life without damaging our view of God's character, we do not yet know Him.

— Oswald Chambers[44]

Question to Consider

What is one thing God might want you to unlearn today?

Prayer

Father, I confess that when difficulties and trials come into my life, large or small, I mostly grumble and complain. I realize the trials James talks about are not necessarily "walls," but they are difficult to bear nonetheless. Fill me with such a vision of a transformed life, O God, that I might actually consider it "pure joy" when you bring trials my way. I believe, Lord. Help my unbelief. In Jesus' name, amen.

Conclude with Silence (2 minutes)

DAY 5: MIDDAY/EVENING OFFICE

Silence, Stillness, and Centering before God (2 minutes)

Scripture Reading: Matthew 26:50b – 53

Then the men stepped forward, seized Jesus and arrested him. With that, one of Jesus' companions reached for his sword, drew it out and struck the servant of the high priest, cutting off his ear.

"Put your sword back in its place," Jesus said to him, "for all who draw the sword will die by the sword. Do you think I cannot call on my Father, and he will at once put at my disposal more than twelve legions of angels?"

Devotional

Walls are sometimes God's way of saying no. The Gospel of John tells us it was the apostle Peter who drew his sword to defend Jesus by force. Peter found it very difficult to accept Jesus' no to his plan for a life and future without a crucifixion. In contrast, we observe David accepting God's no to his desire to build the Temple (2 Samuel 7). Additionally, we read of Jesus submitting to his Father's no — that the cup of the cross be taken from him (Matthew 26:37 – 44).

You may want to use the following prayer of an unknown Confederate soldier to help you embrace God's response when he says yes or no in your journey with him:

> I asked God for strength that I might achieve,
> I was made weak that I might learn to obey.
> I asked for health that I might do great things.
> I was given infirmity that I might do better things.
> I asked for riches that I might be happy;
> I was given poverty that I might be wise.
> I asked for power when I was young that I might
>   have the praise of men;
> I was given weakness that I might feel the need for God.
> I asked for all things that I might enjoy life;
> I was given life that I might enjoy all things.
> Almost despite myself, my unspoken prayers were answered.
> I am, among all people, most richly blessed.

Questions to Consider

Which words speak to you the most from the above prayer? Why?

Prayer

Lord, I relate to Peter's headstrong nature, and to his struggle to understand what you were telling him. It is difficult for me to understand how you are running the universe and my place in it. Transform my stubborn will, O Lord. Teach me to wait on you. Help me to trust you. In Jesus' name, amen.

Conclude with Silence (2 minutes)

Enlarge Your Soul
through Grief and Loss

DAY 1: MORNING/MIDDAY OFFICE

Silence, Stillness, and Centering before God (2 minutes)

Scripture Reading: Matthew 26:36 – 39

Then Jesus went with his disciples to a place called Gethsemane, and he said to them, "Sit here while I go over there and pray." He took Peter and the two sons of Zebedee along with him, and he began to be sorrowful and troubled. Then he said to them, "My soul is overwhelmed with sorrow to the point of death. Stay here and keep watch with me."

Going a little farther, he fell with his face to the ground and prayed, "My Father, if it is possible, may this cup be taken from me. Yet not as I will, but as you will."

Devotional

In the garden of Gethsemane, we see Jesus troubled and overwhelmed with sorrow — to the point of death. We see him falling with his face to the ground and praying three times. We also see the Father say no to Jesus' request that the cup be taken away from him.

We want to follow Jesus into the abundant life of resurrection, but we are less than enthusiastic about following him into the garden of Gethsemane.

Lament for a Son, by Nicholas Wolterstorff, is a record of the author's reflections and struggles following the death of his twenty-five-year-old son, Eric, in an Austrian mountain-climbing accident. Wolterstorff doesn't have any explanations or answers for why God would have allowed such a tragedy. Who does? At one point, however, he comes upon a profound insight:

Through the prism of my tears I have seen a suffering God.

It is said of God that no one can behold his face and live. I always thought this meant that no one can see his splendor and live. A friend said perhaps this meant that no one could see his sorrow and live. Or perhaps his sorrow is splendor.[45]

Question to Consider

What does it mean for you to pray, "Yet not as I will, but as you will"?

Prayer

Lord, everything in me resists following you into the garden of Gethsemane to fall on my face to the ground before you. Grant me the courage to follow you all the way to the cross, whatever that might mean for my life. And then, by your grace, lead me to resurrection life and power. In Jesus' name, amen.

Conclude with Silence (2 minutes)

DAY 1: MIDDAY/EVENING OFFICE

Silence, Stillness, and Centering before God (2 minutes)

Scripture Reading: Job 2:7 – 10

So Satan went out from the presence of the LORD and afflicted Job with painful sores from the soles of his feet to the crown of his head. Then Job took a piece of broken pottery and scraped himself with it as he sat among the ashes.

His wife said to him, "Are you still maintaining your integrity? Curse God and die!"

He replied, "You are talking like a foolish woman. Shall we accept good from God, and not trouble?"

In all this, Job did not sin in what he said.

Devotional

Jonathan Edwards, in a famous sermon on the book of Job, noted that the story of Job is the story of us all. Job lost everything in one day: his family, his wealth, and his health. Most of us experience our losses more slowly — over the span of a lifetime — until we find ourselves on the door of death, leaving everything behind.[46]

> Catastrophic loss by definition precludes recovery. It will transform us or destroy us, but it will never leave us the same. There is no going back to the past....
>
> It is not therefore true that we become less through loss — unless we allow the loss to make us less, grinding our soul down until there is nothing left.... Loss can also make us more....
>
> I did not get over the loss of my loved ones; rather, I absorbed the loss into my life, until it became part of who I am. Sorrow took up permanent residence in my soul and enlarged it....
>
> One learns the pain of others by suffering one's own pain, by turning inside oneself, by finding one's own soul....
>
> However painful, sorrow is good for the soul....
>
> The soul is elastic, like a balloon. It can grow larger through suffering.
>
> — Jerry Sittser[47]

Question to Consider

How can you see God enlarging your soul through your losses?

Prayer

Father, when I think about my losses, it can feel like I have no skin to protect me. I feel raw, scraped to the bone. Looking at Job and Jesus helps, but I must admit that I struggle to see something new being birthed out of the old. Enlarge my soul through the trials and losses of my life. In Jesus' name, amen.

Conclude with Silence (2 minutes)

DAY 2: MORNING/MIDDAY OFFICE

Silence, Stillness, and Centering before God (2 minutes)

Scripture Reading: 2 Corinthians 4:7 – 11

> But we have this treasure in jars of clay to show that this all-surpassing power is from God and not from us. We are hard pressed on every side, but not crushed; perplexed, but not in despair; persecuted, but not abandoned; struck down, but not destroyed. We always carry around in our body the death of Jesus, so that the life of Jesus may also be revealed in our body. For we who are alive are always being given over to death for Jesus' sake, so that his life may also be revealed in our mortal body.

Devotional

Joni Eareckson Tada has been paralyzed from the neck down for over thirty years. As a result, she has experienced both the death of Jesus and the life of Jesus. She says:

> The cross is the center of our relationship with Jesus. The cross is where we die. We go there daily. It isn't easy.
>
> Normally, we will follow Christ anywhere — to a party, as it were, where he changes water into wine, to a sunlit beach where he preaches from a boat. But to the cross? We dig in our heels. The invitation is so frighteningly individual. It's an invitation to go alone.
>
> Suffering reduces us to nothing and as Soren Kierkegaard noted, "God creates everything out of nothing. And everything which God is to use, he first reduces to nothing." To be reduced to nothing is to be dragged to the foot of the cross. It's a severe mercy.

When suffering forces us to our knees at the foot of Calvary, we die to self. We cannot kneel there for long without releasing our pride and anger, unclasping our dreams and desires.... In exchange, God imparts power and implants new and lasting hope.[48]

Question to Consider

How is God bringing you to your knees before him through difficulties and setbacks in your life?

Prayer

Lord, everything in me kicks against going to the foot of the cross where you will root out of me all that is not of you. Help me not to fear the "deaths" it will take for me to be transformed into a free person who loves you and others well. Have mercy on me, O Lord. In Jesus' name, amen.

Conclude with Silence (2 minutes)

DAY 2: MIDDAY/EVENING OFFICE

Silence, Stillness, and Centering before God (2 minutes)

Scripture Reading: Psalm 22:1 – 5

My God, my God, why have you forsaken me?
Why are you so far from saving me,
so far from my cries of anguish?
My God, I cry out by day, but you do not answer,
by night, but I find no rest.
Yet you are enthroned as the Holy One;
you are the one Israel praises.

In you our ancestors put their trust;
    they trusted and you delivered them.
To you they cried out and were saved;
    in you they trusted and were not put to shame.

Devotional

In the 1870s Horatio Spafford was a successful Chicago lawyer and a close friend of evangelist Dwight L. Moody. Spafford had invested heavily in real estate, but the Chicago fire of 1871 wiped out his holdings. His son had died shortly before the disaster. Spafford and his family desperately needed a rest, so in 1873 he planned a trip to Europe with his wife, Anna, and their four daughters. Yet just before they set sail, a last-minute business development forced Horatio to return to work. Not wanting to ruin the family holiday, Spafford persuaded his family to go as planned, and intended to catch up with them later.

With this decided, Spafford returned to Chicago, and Anna and the four daughters sailed to Europe. Unfortunately, their ship collided with an English vessel and sank in only twelve minutes. The accident claimed the lives of 226 people. Anna Spafford had stood bravely on the deck, with her daughters (Annie, Maggie, Bessie, and Tanetta) desperately clinging to her. Her last memory of the disaster is that of her baby being violently torn from her arms by the force of the waters. Just nine days later, Spafford received a telegram from his wife in Wales. It read: "Saved alone." When Horatio Spafford made the ocean crossing to meet his grieving wife, he sailed near the place where his four daughters had sunk to the ocean's depths. There, in the midst of his sorrow, he wrote "It Is Well with My Soul." The words of Staffords's hymn have brought comfort to so many in grief:

When peace, like a river, attendeth my way,
When sorrows like sea-billows roll,
Whatever my lot, Thou hast taught me to say,
It is well, it is well, with my soul.

Though Satan should buffet, though trials should come,
Let this blessed assurance control,
That Christ hath regarded my helpless estate,
And hath shed His own blood for my soul.[49]

Question to Consider

What about Spafford and his relationship with Christ moves you
the most?

Prayer

*Father, I can only bow to you before such unimaginable loss and
suffering. I join with Spafford and pray to you: "Whatever my lot,
Thou has taught me to say, It is well, it is well, with my soul." In
your Son's name, amen.*

Conclude with Silence (2 minutes)

DAY 3: MORNING/MIDDAY OFFICE

Silence, Stillness, and Centering before God (2 minutes)

Scripture Reading: Ecclesiastes 3:1 – 8

There is a time for everything,
and a season for every activity under the heavens:

a time to be born and a time to die,
a time to plant and a time to uproot,
a time to kill and a time to heal,

> a time to tear down and a time to build,
> a time to weep and a time to laugh,
> a time to mourn and a time to dance,
> a time to scatter stones and a time to gather them,
> a time to embrace and a time to refrain from embracing,
> a time to search and a time to give up,
> a time to keep and a time to throw away,
> a time to tear and a time to mend,
> a time to be silent and a time to speak,
> a time to love and a time to hate,
> a time for war and a time for peace.

Devotional

We don't control the seasons; they happen to us. Winter, spring, summer, and fall come to us whether we like it or not. Their rhythms teach us about our spiritual lives and the ways of God. Consider the following description of the paradox of death and rebirth in nature and in our lives:

> Autumn is a season of great beauty, but it is also a season of decline: the days grow shorter, the light is suffused, and summer's abundance decays toward winter's death.... In my own experience of autumn, I am rarely aware that seeds are being planted.... But as I explore autumn's paradox of dying and seeding, I feel the power of metaphor. In the autumnal events of my own experience, I am easily fixated on surface appearances — on the decline of meaning, the decay of relationships, the death of a work. And yet if I look more deeply, I may see the myriad possibilities being planted to bear fruit in some season yet to come.
>
> In retrospect, I can see in my own life what I could not see at the time — how the job I lost helped me find work I needed

to do, how the "road closed" sign turned me toward terrain I needed to travel, how losses that felt irredeemable forced me to discern meanings I needed to know. On the surface it seemed that life was lessening, but silently and lavishly the seeds of new life were always being sown.

— Parker Palmer[50]

Question to Consider

What "road closed" sign is before you today that may be God's way of redirecting you to something new?

Prayer

Lord, grant me wisdom and prudence to see the larger picture, to wait, and to discern the seasons in my life with you. Forgive me for fighting the "deaths" you send into my life in order to plant something new. In Jesus' name, amen.

Conclude with Silence (2 minutes)

DAY 3: MIDDAY/EVENING OFFICE

Silence, Stillness, and Centering before God (2 minutes)

Scripture Reading: John 3:26 – 30

They came to John and said to him, "Rabbi, that man who was with you on the other side of the Jordan — the one you testified about — look, he is baptizing, and everyone is going to him."

To this John replied, "A person can receive only what is given them from heaven. You yourselves can testify that I said, 'I am not the Messiah but am sent ahead of him.' The bride belongs to the bridegroom. The friend who attends the bride-groom waits and listens for him, and is full of joy when he hears the bridegroom's voice. That joy is mine, and it is now complete. He must become greater; I must become less."

Devotional

Experiencing loss makes us confront our humanity and our limits. We quickly realize we are not in control of our lives; God is. We are simply creatures, not the Creator.

Consider the example of John the Baptist. Crowds that formerly followed John for baptism switched their allegiances once Jesus began his ministry. They began leaving John to follow Jesus. Some of John's followers were upset about this dramatic turn of events. They complained to him, "Everyone is going to him" (John 3:26).

John understood limits and replied, "A person can receive only what is given them from heaven" (John 3:27). He was able to accept his limits, his humanity, and his declining popularity and say, "He must become greater; I must become less" (John 3:30).

Getting off of our thrones and joining the rest of humanity is a must if we are to develop spiritual maturity. We are not the center of the universe. The universe does not revolve around us.

Yet a part of us hates limits. We won't accept them. This is one of the primary reasons that biblically grieving our losses is such an indispensable part of spiritual maturity.

Embracing our limits humbles us like little else.[51]

Question to Consider

Name one or two limits God has recently placed in your life as a gift.

Prayer

> *Lord, forgive me for the arrogance that sees interruptions to my plans as alien invasions. Forgive me for constantly trying to do more than you intend with my life. Help me to be like John the Baptist, embracing my losses and respecting my limits. In Jesus' name, amen.*

Conclude with Silence (2 minutes)

DAY 4: MORNING/MIDDAY OFFICE

Silence, Stillness, and Centering before God (2 minutes)

Scripture Reading: 2 Samuel 1:17 – 20, 24 – 25 (NIV 1984)

David took up this lament concerning Saul and his son Jonathan, and ordered that the men of Judah be taught this lament of the bow (it is written in the Book of Jashar):

"Your glory, O Israel, lies slain on your heights.
　　How the mighty have fallen!
"Tell it not in Gath,
　　proclaim it not in the streets of Ashkelon,
lest the daughters of the Philistines be glad,
　　lest the daughters of the uncircumcised rejoice.
"Daughters of Israel,
　　weep for Saul,
who clothed you in scarlet and finery,
　　who adorned your garments with ornaments of gold.
"How the mighty have fallen in battle!
　　Jonathan lies slain on your heights."

Devotional

David not only sang this lamentation, but he also ordered the people to learn it, memorize it, and inhabit it as their experience.

> Pain isn't the worst thing. Being hated isn't the worst thing. Being separated from the one you love isn't the worst thing. Death isn't the worst thing. The worst thing is failing to deal with reality and becoming disconnected from what is actual. The worst thing is trivializing the honorable, desecrating the sacred. What I do with my grief affects the way you handle your grief; together we form a community that deals with death and other loss in the context of God's sovereignty, which is expressed finally in resurrection....
>
> We don't become mature human beings by getting lucky or cleverly circumventing loss, and certainly not by avoidance and distraction. Learn to lament. Learn this lamentation. We're mortals, after all. We and everyone around are scheduled for death (mortis). Get used to it. Take up your cross. It prepares us and those around us for resurrection.
>
> — Eugene Peterson[52]

Question to Consider

What might it mean for you to mature by entering the painful reality of your losses rather than avoiding them?

Prayer

Lord, I have spent much of my life running from pain and loss, medicating my pain and quickly moving on to the next project — the new urgent demand. I ask for the grace to embrace all of life — the joys and the sorrows, the deaths and the births, the old and the new. In Jesus' name, amen.

Conclude with Silence (2 minutes)

DAY 4: MIDDAY/EVENING OFFICE

Silence, Stillness, and Centering before God (2 minutes)

Scripture Reading: Luke 19:41 – 44

As he approached Jerusalem and saw the city, he wept over it and said, "If you, even you, had only known on this day what would bring you peace — but now it is hidden from your eyes. The days will come upon you when your enemies will build an embankment against you and encircle you and hem you in on every side. They will dash you to the ground, you and the children within your walls. They will not leave one stone on another, because you did not recognize the time of God's coming to you."

Devotional

The Greek word used to describe Jesus weeping over Jerusalem is that of a person wailing or sobbing. Imagine the scene!

Sadly, many of us, unlike our Lord, feel guilty expressing raw feelings such as sadness and anger. The problem is that when we deny our pain, losses, and feelings year after year, we transform slowly into empty shells with smiley faces painted on them. But when we begin to allow ourselves to feel a wider range of emotions (including sadness, depression, fear, and anger), a profound change takes place in our relationship with God. As Ken Gire wrote:

> C. S. Lewis said that "we should bring to God what is in us, not what ought to be in us." The "oughts" will keep us from telling the truth. They will also keep us from feeling the truth. Especially the truth about our pain....
>
> When Jesus realized the nearness of His own death, He went to a quiet place and prayed.... We are told that He agonized

with "loud crying and tears" (Heb. 5:7). We are also told that He fell to the ground, where He prayed fervently and sweated profusely (Luke 22:44).

This was no Renaissance painting. This was a real portrait, a portrait of how we pray when the earth beneath our feet begins to quake. We pray however we can, with whatever words we can. We pray with our sweat, with our tears. And with whatever friends we have who will sit with us in the darkness.[53]

Question to Consider

How would it change your prayer life to bring to God what is actually in you and not what you think ought to be in you?

Prayer

Abba Father, I admit that I am often afraid and embarrassed to openly tell you all that is going on inside me — even though I know you know it all anyway. Teach me what boldness in prayer looks like as I draw near your throne of grace. In Jesus' name, amen.

Conclude with Silence (2 minutes)

DAY 5: MORNING/MIDDAY OFFICE

Silence, Stillness, and Centering before God (2 minutes)

Scripture Reading: Hebrews 5:7 – 8

During the days of Jesus' life on earth, he offered up prayers and petitions with fervent cries and tears to the one who could save him from death, and he was heard because of his reverent submission. Son though he was, he learned obedience from what he suffered.

Devotional

The capacity to grieve is almost lost in our culture. People use work, TV, drugs, alcohol, shopping, food binges, busyness, sexual escapades, unhealthy relationships, and even serving others at church — anything — to medicate the pain of life. Year after year we deny and avoid the difficulties and losses of life, the rejections and frustrations. When a loss enters our life we become angry at God and treat it as an alien invasion from outer space.

This is unbiblical and a denial of our common humanity. Consider the following examples: The ancient Hebrews physically expressed their laments by tearing their clothes and utilizing sackcloth and ashes. Jesus himself offered up "prayer and petitions with fervent cries and tears." During Noah's generation, God was grieved about the state of humanity (Genesis 6). Jeremiah wrote six confessions or laments in which he protested to God about his circumstances. Then, after the fall of Jerusalem, he wrote an entire book called Lamentations.

The God-like response to loss is neither spin nor a cover-up. Scripture teaches us to deal honestly and prayerfully with our losses and disappointments (big and small), and all their accompanying confusing emotions. Why? Losses are indispensable if we are going to change and grow into the men and women God has called us to be.[54]

Question to Consider

In what ways are you tempted to spin or cover over your losses and miss God's deeper work in you?

Prayer

Lord, I acknowledge that I prefer to ignore and deny my pain and loss. I struggle with seeing how resurrection life can come out of death. Grant me the courage to pay attention to what you are doing, and to wait on you — even when everything in me wants to run away. In Jesus' name, amen.

Conclude with Silence (2 minutes)

DAY 5: MIDDAY/EVENING OFFICE

Silence, Stillness, and Centering before God (2 minutes)

Scripture Reading: Job 42:12 – 17

The LORD blessed the latter part of Job's life more than the former part. He had fourteen thousand sheep, six thousand camels, a thousand yoke of oxen and a thousand donkeys. And he also had seven sons and three daughters. The first daughter he named Jemimah, the second Keziah and the third Keren-Happuch. Nowhere in all the land were there found women as beautiful as Job's daughters, and their father granted them an inheritance along with their brothers.

After this, Job lived a hundred and forty years; he saw his children and their children to the fourth generation. And so Job died, an old man and full of years.

Devotional

Good grieving is not just letting go, but also letting the loss bless us. Job did just that.

The old life for Job was truly over. That door remained closed. That is the source of the great grief that arises from our losses. There is finality. We can't get what we've lost back. Yet if we follow Job's path, we will be blessed. That is one of the major lessons of Job. He followed the difficult path of allowing his losses to enlarge his soul for God, and God blessed him superabundantly. Not only was Job spiritually transformed, but the Lord blessed him with new prosperity. His wealth was doubled, God gave him ten children once again, and he lived to a ripe old age.

This account is meant to encourage us to trust the living God with the many mini-deaths that we experience in our lives. The central message of Christ is that suffering and death bring resurrection and transformation. Jesus himself said, "I tell you the truth, unless a kernel of wheat falls to the ground and dies, it remains only a single seed. But if it dies, it produces many seeds" (John 12:24 NIV 1984).

But remember, resurrection only comes out of death — real death. Our losses are real, and so is our God — the living God.[55]

Question to Consider

How is God coming to you through the "mini-deaths" in your life now?

Prayer

Lord, after his loss, you gave Job prosperity, blessing him with twice as much as he had before, but that has not always felt like my experience. Grant me patience. Help me to trust and wait on you, especially in those areas of my life where I have no idea what you are doing, when my hardship will end, or where you are taking me. In Jesus' name, amen.

Conclude with Silence (2 minutes)

Discover the Rhythms of the Daily Office and Sabbath

DAY 1: MORNING/MIDDAY OFFICE

Silence, Stillness, and Centering before God (2 minutes)

Scripture Reading: Luke 8:11 – 15

"This is the meaning of the parable: The seed is the word of God. Those along the path are the ones who hear, and then the devil comes and takes away the word from their hearts, so that they may not believe and be saved. Those on the rocky ground are the ones who receive the word with joy when they hear it, but they have no root. They believe for a while, but in the time of testing they fall away. The seed that fell among thorns stands for those who hear, but as they go on their way they are choked by life's worries, riches and pleasures, and they do not mature. But the seed on good soil stands for those with a noble and good heart, who hear the word, retain it, and by persevering produce a crop."

Devotional

Awareness of the love of God — and responding to it — is at the heart of our lives.

> Every moment and every event of every man's life on earth plants something in his soul. For just as the wind carries thousands of winged seeds, so each moment brings with it germs of spiritual vitality that come to rest imperceptibly in the minds and wills of men. Most of these unnumbered seeds perish and are lost, because men are not prepared to receive them: for such seeds as these cannot spring up anywhere except in the good soil of freedom, spontaneity and love.
>
> This is no new idea. Christ in the parable of the sower

long ago told us that "The seed is the word of God." We often think this applies only to the word of the Gospel as formally preached in churches on Sundays.... But every expression of the will of God is in some sense a "word" of God and therefore a "seed" of new life. The ever-changing reality in the midst of which we live should awaken us to the possibility of an uninterrupted dialogue with God....

We must learn to realize that the love of God seeks us in every situation, and seeks our good.

— Thomas Merton[56]

Question to Consider

Pause and consider your day. What seeds from God might be coming to you that you don't want to miss?

Prayer

Lord, I praise you because your love seeks my good in any and every situation. Forgive me for the seeds that I have squandered. Soften my heart to surrender to your will in and through me. In Jesus' name, amen.

Conclude with Silence (2 minutes)

DAY 1: MIDDAY/EVENING OFFICE

Silence, Stillness, and Centering before God (2 minutes)

Scripture Reading: Genesis 2:9b, 15 – 17

In the middle of the garden were the tree of life and the tree of the knowledge of good and evil.

The LORD God took the man and put him in the Garden

of Eden to work it and take care of it. And the LORD God commanded the man, "You are free to eat from any tree in the garden; but you must not eat from the tree of the knowledge of good and evil, for when you eat from it you will certainly die."

Devotional

At the heart of the Daily Office and Sabbath disciplines is stopping to surrender to God in trust. Lack of trust is the very essence of the sin in the garden of Eden. Adam and Eve legitimately worked and enjoyed their achievements in the garden. However, they were called to embrace their limits and not eat from the tree of the knowledge of good and evil. They were not meant to see and know that which belongs to Almighty God.

As theologian Robert Barron has argued, the heart of the original sin is the refusal to accept God's rhythm for us. The essence of being created in God's image is our ability, like God, to stop. We imitate God by stopping our work and resting. If we can stop for one day a week, or for a mini-Sabbath each day (a Daily Office), we touch something deep within us as image bearers of God. Our brains, bodies, spirits, and emotions are all wired by God for the rhythm of working and resting in him.

Stopping for a Daily Office or the Sabbath is not meant to add another obligation to our already busy schedules. It is an entirely new way of being in the world, resetting all of our days toward a new destination — God.[57]

Question to Consider

How do you hear the invitation to "stop and surrender to God in trust" today?

Prayer

> *Lord, help me to grab hold of you today. I need you. Set me free*
> *to begin reorienting my life around you, and you alone. Help me*
> *to pay attention to and honor how you have uniquely made me.*
> *Thank you for the gift of rest. In Jesus' name, amen.*

Conclude with Silence (2 minutes)

DAY 2: MORNING/MIDDAY OFFICE

Silence, Stillness, and Centering before God (2 minutes)

Scripture Reading: 1 Kings 19:11 – 12

The LORD said, "Go out and stand on the mountain in the presence of the LORD, for the LORD is about to pass by."

Then a great and powerful wind tore the mountains apart and shattered the rocks before the LORD, but the LORD was not in the wind. After the wind there was an earthquake, but the LORD was not in the earthquake. After the earthquake came a fire, but the LORD was not in the fire. And after the fire came a gentle whisper.

Devotional

When God appeared to Elijah (after his flight from Jezebel and during his suicidal depression), he told him to stand and wait for the presence of the Lord to pass by. God did not appear in ways he had showed up in the past. God was not in the wind (as with Job), an earthquake (as when he gave the Ten Commandments on Mount Sinai), or fire (like the burning bush Moses saw). God revealed himself to Elijah in "a gentle whisper," which can also be translated as "a sound of sheer silence." The common translation of this passage does not fully capture the original Hebrew, but what could the translators do? How do you hear silence?

The silence after the chaos, for Elijah and for us, is full of the presence of God. God spoke to Elijah out of the silence.[58]

God invites you to stand and to wait like Elijah. Why? God also wants to speak to you out of the "sound of sheer silence."

Question to Consider

When can you set aside some time for extended, uninterrupted silence to hear God?

Prayer

Lord, you know how difficult it is for me to be in silence before you. At times it feels almost impossible, given the demands, distractions, and noise all around me. I invite you to lead me to a quiet, silent place before you — to a place where I can hear you as Elijah did. In Jesus' name, amen.

Conclude with Silence (2 minutes)

DAY 2: MIDDAY/EVENING OFFICE

Silence, Stillness, and Centering before God (2 minutes)

Scripture Reading: John 15:4 – 6

"Remain in me, as I also remain in you. No branch can bear fruit by itself; it must remain in the vine. Neither can you bear fruit unless you remain in me.

"I am the vine; you are the branches. If you remain in me and I in you, you will bear much fruit; apart from me you can do nothing. If you do not remain in me, you are like a branch that is thrown away and withers; such branches are picked up, thrown into the fire and burned."

Devotional

When we are busier than God requires us to be, we do violence to ourselves. Thomas Merton understood this and wrote:

> There is a pervasive form of contemporary violence ... activism and overwork. The rush and pressure of modern life are a form, perhaps the most common form, of its innate violence. To allow oneself to be carried away by a multitude of conflicting concerns, to surrender to too many demands. To commit oneself to too many projects, to want to help everyone in everything, is to succumb to violence. The frenzy ... kills the root of inner wisdom which makes work fruitful.[59]

And when we do this violence to ourselves, we are unable to love others in and through the love of Christ.

Question to Consider

In what ways are you busier than God requires?

Prayer

Father, I know how often I am carried away by too many concerns and demands and projects. I have felt the violence to my soul. Deliver me from this whirlwind around me and in me. Heal my tired and weary spirit, allowing the wisdom that comes from rest in you to flow deep within me. In Jesus' name, amen.

Conclude with Silence (2 minutes)

DAY 3: MORNING/MIDDAY OFFICE

Silence, Stillness, and Centering before God (2 minutes)

Scripture Reading: Psalm 46:1 – 3, 10

> God is our refuge and strength,
> an ever-present help in trouble.

Therefore we will not fear, though the earth give way
    and the mountains fall into the heart of the sea,
though its waters roar and foam
    and the mountains quake with their surging.
He says, "Be still, and know that I am God;
    I will be exalted among the nations,
    I will be exalted in the earth."

Devotional

Many are avidly seeking but they alone find who remain in continual silence.... Every man who delights in a multitude of words, even though he says admirable things, is empty within. If you love truth, be a lover of silence. Silence like the sunlight will illuminate you in God and will deliver you from the phantoms of ignorance. Silence will unite you to God himself....

More than all things love silence: it brings you a fruit that tongue cannot describe. In the beginning we have to force ourselves to be silent. But then there is born something that draws us to silence. May God give you an experience of this "something" that is born of silence. If only you practice this, untold light will dawn on you in consequence ... after a while a certain sweetness is born in the heart of this exercise and the body is drawn almost by force to remain in silence.

— Isaac of Nineveh[60]

Question to Consider

What keeps you from silence?

Prayer

Lord, help me to be still and to wait patiently for you in silence. In Jesus' name, amen.

Conclude with Silence (2 minutes)

DAY 3: MIDDAY/EVENING OFFICE

Silence, Stillness, and Centering before God (2 minutes)

Scripture Reading: Matthew 13:31 – 33

> He told them another parable: "The kingdom of heaven is like a mustard seed, which a man took and planted in his field. Though it is the smallest of all seeds, yet when it grows, it is the largest of garden plants and becomes a tree, so that the birds come and perch in its branches."
>
> He told them still another parable: "The kingdom of heaven is like yeast that a woman took and mixed into about sixty pounds of flour until it worked all through the dough."

Devotional

In these two parables describing the kingdom of God, we hear Jesus calling us to slow down and take a longer view of our lives.

> We can work without stopping, faster and faster, electric lights making artificial day so the whole machine can labor without ceasing. But remember: No living thing lives like this. There are greater rhythms that govern how life grows: seasons and sunsets and great movements of seas and stars.... We are part of the creation story, subject to all its laws and rhythms.
>
> To surrender to the rhythms of seasons and flowerings and dormancies is to savor the secret of life itself.
>
> Many scientists believe we are "hard-wired" like this, to live in rhythmic awareness, to be in and then step out, to be engrossed and then detached, to work and then to rest. It follows then that the commandment to remember the Sabbath is not a burdensome requirement from some law-giving deity — "You ought, you'd better, you must" — but rather a remem-

brance of a law that is firmly embedded in the fabric of nature. It is a reminder of how things really are, the rhythmic dance to which we unavoidably belong.

— Wayne Muller[61]

Question to Consider

How do the rhythms you see in nature (e.g., spring, summer, fall, winter, day, night) speak to you and point to the kind of rhythms you desire for your own life?

Prayer

Lord, I thank you that you are working even when I am sleeping. Teach me to respect the built-in rhythms of life, and to live from a place of deep rest in you. In Jesus' name, amen.

Conclude with Silence (2 minutes)

DAY 4: MORNING/MIDDAY OFFICE

Silence, Stillness, and Centering before God (2 minutes)

Scripture Reading: Mark 2:23 – 28

One Sabbath Jesus was going through the grainfields, and as his disciples walked along, they began to pick some heads of grain. The Pharisees said to him, "Look, why are they doing what is unlawful on the Sabbath?"

He answered, "Have you never read what David did when he and his companions were hungry and in need? In the days of Abiathar the high priest, he entered the house of God and ate the consecrated bread, which is lawful only for priests to eat. And he also gave some to his companions."

Then he said to them, "The Sabbath was made for man,

not man for the Sabbath. So the Son of Man is Lord even of the Sabbath."

Devotional

Sabbath is not dependent upon our readiness to stop. We do not stop when we are finished. We do not stop when we complete our phone calls, finish our project, get through this stack of messages, or get out this report that is due tomorrow. We stop because it is time to stop.

Sabbath requires surrender. If we only stop when we are finished with all our work, we will never stop — because our work is never completely done. With every accomplishment there arises a new responsibility.... If we refuse rest until we are finished, we will never rest until we die. Sabbath dissolves the artificial urgency of our days, because it liberates us from the need to be finished....

We stop because there are forces larger than we that take care of the universe, and while our efforts are important, necessary, and useful, they are not (nor are we) indispensable. The galaxy will somehow manage without us for this hour, this day, and so we are invited — nay, commanded — to relax, and enjoy our relative unimportance, our humble place at the table in a very large world....

Do not be anxious about tomorrow, Jesus said again and again. Let the work of this day be sufficient....

Sabbath says, Be still. Stop. There is no rush to get to the end, because we are never finished.

— Wayne Muller[62]

Question to Consider

What is your greatest fear in stopping for a twenty-four-hour period each week?

Prayer

> *Keeping the Sabbath, Lord, will require a lot of changes in the way I am living life. Teach me, Lord, how to take the next step with this in a way that fits my unique personality and situation. Help me to trust you with all that will remain unfinished and to enjoy my humble place in your very large world. In Jesus' name, amen.*

Conclude with Silence (2 minutes)

DAY 4: MIDDAY/EVENING OFFICE

Silence, Stillness, and Centering before God (2 minutes)

Scripture Reading: Psalm 92:1 – 6

> It is good to praise the LORD
>   and make music to your name, O Most High,
> proclaiming your love in the morning
>   and your faithfulness at night,
> to the music of the ten-stringed lyre
>   and the melody of the harp.
>
> For you make me glad by your deeds, LORD;
>   I sing for joy at what your hands have done.
> How great are your works, LORD,
>   how profound your thoughts!
> Senseless people do not know,
>   fools do not understand.

Devotional

Psalm 92 is a song that was intended for the Sabbath. It stands as an indictment against today's culture of exhaustion and destruction. It also presents us with a positive vision of observing the Sabbath that takes us far beyond a mere reprieve from six days of frantic exertion. Sabbath is the focus and culmination of a life that is daily and practically devoted to honoring God.

> Abraham Joshua Heschel once observed, "Unless one learns how to relish the taste of Sabbath while still in this world, unless one is initiated in the appreciation of eternal life, one will be unable to enjoy the taste of eternity in the world to come." We are simply naïve if we think that having wasted or squandered the many good gifts of this creation, we will not do the same with the gifts of heaven. Sabbath practice, on this view, is a sort of training ground for the life of eternity, a preparation for the full reception and welcome of the presence of God.
>
> — Norman Wirzba[63]

Question to Consider

How might Sabbath keeping (for an entire twenty-four-hour period) or practicing the Daily Office (a mini-Sabbath for a few minutes) provide you with a taste of eternity?

Prayer

Lord, show me how to welcome your presence, not only one day a week, but every day. Train me for eternity. Grant me a taste of heaven through the experience of true Sabbath rest. In Jesus' name, amen.

Conclude with Silence (2 minutes)

DAY 5: MORNING/MIDDAY OFFICE

Silence, Stillness, and Centering before God (2 minutes)

Scripture Reading: Psalm 23:1 – 3

The LORD is my shepherd, I lack nothing.
    He makes me lie down in green pastures,
he leads me beside quiet waters,
    he refreshes my soul.
He guides me along the right paths
    for his name's sake.

Devotional

The Sabbath teaches us grace because it connects us experientially to the basic truth that nothing we do will earn God's love. As long as we are working hard, using our gifts to serve others, experiencing joy in our work along with the toil, we are always in danger of believing that our actions trigger God's love for us. Only in stopping, really stopping, do we teach our hearts and souls that we are loved apart from what we do.

During a day of rest, we have the chance to take a deep breath and look at our lives. God is at work every minute of our days, yet we seldom notice. Noticing requires intentional stopping, and the Sabbath provides that opportunity. On the Sabbath we can take a moment to see the beauty of a maple leaf, created with great care by our loving Creator....

Without time to stop, we cannot notice God's hand in our lives, practice thankfulness, step outside our culture's values or explore our deepest longings. Without time to rest, we will seriously undermine our ability to experience God's unconditional love and acceptance. The Sabbath is a gift whose blessings cannot be found anywhere else.

— Lynne Baab[64]

Question to Consider

How will you allow God to lead you to the "quiet waters" of rest this week so that you experience his unconditional love and acceptance?

Prayer

> *Lord, I now take a deep breath and stop. So often I miss your hand and gifts in my life because I am preoccupied and anxious. Grant me the power to pause each day and each week to simply rest in your arms of love. In Jesus' name, amen.*

Conclude with Silence (2 minutes)

DAY 5: MIDDAY/EVENING OFFICE

Silence, Stillness, and Centering before God (2 minutes)

Scripture Reading: Deuteronomy 5:12 – 15

"Observe the Sabbath day by keeping it holy, as the LORD your God has commanded you. Six days you shall labor and do all your work, but the seventh day is a sabbath to the LORD your God. On it you shall not do any work, neither you, nor your son or daughter, nor your male or female servant, nor your ox, your donkey or any of your animals, nor any foreigner residing in your towns, so that your male or female servants may rest, as you do. Remember that you were slaves in Egypt and that the LORD your God brought you out of there with a mighty hand and an outstretched arm. Therefore the LORD your God has commanded you to observe the Sabbath day."

Devotional

Sabbath was intended to shape our lives as a liberated people. The fourth commandment calls for a day of rest — even for people who had been enslaved.

The Deuteronomy reason for Sabbath-keeping is that our ancestors in Egypt went for four hundred years without a vacation (Deuteronomy 5:15). Never a day off. The consequence: they were no longer considered persons but slaves. Hands. Work units. Not persons created in the image of God but equipment for making brick and building pyramids. Humanity was defaced.

— Eugene Peterson[65]

Keeping the Sabbaths is meant to be an experience of the truth that you are not a "doing machine," but a deeply loved son or daughter of God. He is not interested in simply using you to get work done; God delights in you. He provides free time once a week so that you might relish your release from all forms of oppression and slavery.

Question to Consider

How might the truth that God doesn't want to use you, but to enjoy you, give you a vision for celebrating the Sabbath?

Prayer

Lord, Sabbath rest is truly an unbelievable gift! Thank you that there is nothing I can do to earn your love; it comes without any strings attached. As I close my eyes for these few minutes before you, all I can say is, thank you! In Jesus' name, amen.

Conclude with Silence (2 minutes)

Grow into an Emotionally Mature Adult

DAY 1: MORNING/MIDDAY OFFICE

Silence, Stillness, and Centering before God (2 minutes)

Scripture Reading: Luke 9:49 – 55

"Master," said John, "we saw someone driving out demons in your name and we tried to stop him, because he is not one of us."

"Do not stop him," Jesus said, "for whoever is not against you is for you."

As the time approached for him to be taken up to heaven, Jesus resolutely set out for Jerusalem. And he sent messengers on ahead, who went into a Samaritan village to get things ready for him; but the people there did not welcome him, because he was heading for Jerusalem. When the disciples James and John saw this, they asked, "Lord, do you want us to call fire down from heaven to destroy them?" But Jesus turned and rebuked them.

Devotional

We often forget that the people Jesus chose to form the leadership of his church were neither spiritually nor emotionally mature. Like us, they had a great deal to learn.

Peter, the point leader, had a big problem with his mouth and was a bundle of contradictions. Andrew, his brother, was quiet and remained behind the scenes. James and John were called "sons of thunder" because they were aggressive, hotheaded, ambitious, and intolerant. Philip was skeptical and negative. He had limited vision. "We can't do that," summed up his lack of faith when confronted by the problem of feeding the five thousand. Nathanael Bartholomew was prejudiced and opinionated. Matthew was the most hated person in Capernaum, working in a profession that abused innocent people. Thomas was melancholy, mildly depressive, and pessimistic. James, son of Alphaeus, and Judas, son of James, were nobodies. The Bible says nothing about them. Simon the Zealot was a freedom fighter and a terrorist in his day. Judas, the treasurer, was a thief and a loner. He pretended to be loyal to Jesus and then betrayed him.

Most of them, however, did have one great quality. They were willing. That is all God asks of us.[66]

Question to Consider

What is one step you can take to place yourself (with all your flaws) in the hands of Jesus, inviting him to mold you into a spiritually and emotionally mature disciple?

Prayer

Lord Jesus, I can relate to the disciples who wanted to call down fire from heaven on the Samaritans and who fought over which of them was the greatest. Forgive my arrogance.

Cleanse me and fill me with your power so that I might love well today for your name's sake. Amen.

Conclude with Silence (2 minutes)

DAY 1: MIDDAY/EVENING OFFICE

Silence, Stillness, and Centering before God (2 minutes)

Scripture Reading: Mark 5:30 – 34

At once Jesus realized that power had gone out from him. He turned around in the crowd and asked, "Who touched my clothes?"

"You see the people crowding against you," his disciples answered, "and yet you can ask, 'Who touched me?'"

But Jesus kept looking around to see who had done it. Then the woman, knowing what had happened to her, came and fell at his feet and, trembling with fear, told him the whole truth. He said to her, "Daughter, your faith has healed you. Go in peace and be freed from your suffering."

Devotional

As emotionally mature Christian adults, we recognize that loving well is the essence of true spirituality. This requires that we experience connection with God, with ourselves, and with other people. God invites us to practice his presence in our daily lives. At the same time, he invites us to "practice the presence of people," within an awareness of his presence, in our daily relationships. Sadly, the two are rarely brought together.

Jesus' profound, contemplative prayer life with his Father resulted in a contemplative presence with people. Love is "to reveal the beauty of another person to themselves," wrote Jean Vanier. Jesus did that with each person he met. We see this in his interaction with the woman suffering from a twelve-year bleeding problem (Mark 5).

This ability to really listen and pay attention to people was at the very heart of Jesus' mission, and it could not help but move him to compassion. In the same way, out of our contemplative time with God, we too are invited to be prayerfully present to people, revealing their beauty to them.

Unfortunately, the religious leaders of Jesus' day, the "church leaders" of that time, never made that connection.[67]

Question to Consider

How can you "practice the presence of people" within an awareness of God's presence today?

Prayer

> *Lord, I have unhealthy ways of relating to others that are deeply imbedded in me. Please change me. Make me a vessel to spread mature, steady, and reliable love so that those I come in contact with will sense your tenderness and kindness through me. In Jesus' name, amen.*

Conclude with Silence (2 minutes)

DAY 2: MORNING/MIDDAY OFFICE

Silence, Stillness, and Centering before God (2 minutes)

Scripture Reading: Luke 15:20b – 24

"But while he was still a long way off, his father saw him and was filled with compassion for him; he ran to his son, threw his arms around him and kissed him.

"The son said to him, 'Father, I have sinned against heaven and against you. I am no longer worthy to be called your son.'

"But the father said to his servants, 'Quick! Bring the best robe and put it on him. Put a ring on his finger and sandals on his feet. Bring the fattened calf and kill it. Let's have a feast and celebrate. For this son of mine was dead and is alive again; he was lost and is found.' So they began to celebrate."

Devotional

In the famous parable of the prodigal son, Jesus' description of the father gives us a glimpse of what it looks like for us to be emotionally mature adults.

The church is full of "younger sons" who wander from the love of God every time he does not meet their expectations. It is also full of "elder brothers" who are angry, bitter, and grumpy. I know them both well. I relate to both.

Yet people are desperately looking for fathers and mothers in the faith who are able to embrace, love, empathize, be present, and forgive freely. It is a love without conditions, something the world knows very little about. To become this kind of person does not come naturally. As Henri Nouwen has written:

> I have to kneel before the Father, put my ear against his chest and listen, without interruption, to the heartbeat of God. Then, and only then, can I say carefully and very gently what I hear. I know now that I have to speak from eternity into time, from the lasting joy into the passing realities of our short existence in this world, from the house of love into the houses of fear, from God's abode into the dwellings of human beings.[68]

Question to Consider

Which words from Nouwen's quotation about the prodigal son speak to you?

Prayer

Father, help me to be still and listen to you, feel your embrace, and rest in your love — and then to speak to others from that place. In Jesus' name, amen.

Conclude with Silence (2 minutes)

DAY 2: MIDDAY/EVENING OFFICE

Silence, Stillness, and Centering before God (2 minutes)

Scripture Reading: Psalm 130

Out of the depths I cry to you, O LORD;
    O Lord, hear my voice.
Let your ears be attentive
    to my cry for mercy.
If you, O LORD, kept a record of sins,
    O Lord, who could stand?
But with you there is forgiveness;
    therefore you are feared.
I wait for the LORD, my soul waits,
    and in his word I put my hope.
My soul waits for the Lord
    more than watchmen wait for the morning
    more than watchmen wait for the morning.
O Israel, put your hope in the LORD,
    for with the LORD is unfailing love
    and with him is full redemption.
He himself will redeem Israel
    from all their sins. (NIV 1984)

Devotional

I am able to "wait for the Lord" for something — a new opportunity, blessings for my children, the healing of a friendship, or a safe trip out of town. It is much more difficult for me to "wait for the Lord" for nothing, but to simply be still before him. Yet this is one of the keys to loving others well.

> Although I often try to pull it off, I know that I cannot really be present for another person when my inner world is filled with preoccupations and distractions. This is one of the biggest challenges I face in being present for others — being still within my own soul. Stillness is the precondition of presence. I must first be still to myself if I am to be still with another. And,

of course, I must learn to be still before God if I am to learn to be still in myself. Presence begins with a still place within one's self. If I have no such still inner place, I cannot really be present for others.

— David Benner[69]

Question to Consider

What is the biggest challenge you face in being still before the Lord?

Prayer

Lord, I confess to you that I am not sure what it looks like to still and quiet my soul before you. Lead me on a journey to discover that still place within myself, and I will follow wherever and however you lead me. In Jesus' name, amen.

Conclude with Silence (2 minutes)

DAY 3: MORNING/MIDDAY OFFICE

Silence, Stillness, and Centering before God (2 minutes)

Scripture Reading: Matthew 25:34 – 36, 40

"Then the King will say to those on his right, 'Come, you who are blessed by my Father; take your inheritance, the kingdom prepared for you since the creation of the world. For I was hungry and you gave me something to eat, I was thirsty and you gave me something to drink, I was a stranger and you invited me in, I needed clothes and you clothed me, I was sick and you looked after me, I was in prison and you came to visit me.'

"The King will reply, 'Truly I tell you, whatever you did for one of the least of these brothers and sisters of mine, you did for me.'"

Devotional

In 1952 Mother Teresa began picking up the dying in the streets of Calcutta, India. By 1980 she and over three thousand members of her order, the Missionaries of Charity, were working in fifty-two countries. Her teachings and life give us profound insight into what it means to follow Jesus as emotional and spiritual adults in our world. She wrote:

> I never look at the masses as my responsibility. I look only at the individual. I can love only one person at a time. I can feed only one person at a time. Just one, one, one. You get closer to Christ by coming closer to each other. As Jesus said, "Whatever you do to the least of my brethren, you do it to me." So you begin ... I begin. I picked up one person.... The whole work is only a drop in the ocean. But if we don't put the drop in, the ocean would be one drop less. Same thing for you. Same thing in your family. Same thing in the church where you go. Just begin ... one, one, one! At the end of our lives, we will not be judged by how many diplomas we have received, how much money we have made or how many great things we have done. We will be judged by "I was hungry and you gave me to eat. I was naked and you clothed me. I was homeless and you took me in."[70]

Question to Consider

How can you begin to see Jesus Christ in the people you meet this week?

Prayer

Lord, I am often overwhelmed by the needs of the world around me. Thank you that you are responsible for the world, and I am not. Help me to see the individual today — the "one, one, one" — so that the words and actions that flow from my life might reflect your life. In Jesus' name, amen.

Conclude with Silence (2 minutes)

DAY 3: MIDDAY/EVENING OFFICE

Silence, Stillness, and Centering before God (2 minutes)

Scripture Reading: Luke 10:30 – 37

In reply Jesus said: "A man was going down from Jerusalem to Jericho, when he was attacked by robbers. They stripped him of his clothes, beat him and went away, leaving him half dead. A priest happened to be going down the same road, and when he saw the man, he passed by on the other side. So too, a Levite, when he came to the place and saw him, passed by on the other side. But a Samaritan, as he traveled, came where the man was; and when he saw him, he took pity on him. He went to him and bandaged his wounds, pouring on oil and wine. Then he put the man on his own donkey, brought him to an inn and took care of him. The next day he took out two denarii and gave them to the innkeeper. 'Look after him,' he said, 'and when I return, I will reimburse you for any extra expense you may have.'

"Which of these three do you think was a neighbor to the man who fell into the hands of robbers?"

The expert in the law replied, "The one who had mercy on him."

Jesus told him, "Go and do likewise."

Devotional

The great Jewish theologian Martin Buber described the healthiest or maturest relationship possible between two human beings as an "I-Thou" relationship. In such a relationship, I recognize that I am made in the image of God, and so is every other person. This makes them a "Thou" to me. They have dignity and worth, and are to be treated with respect. I affirm them as being a unique and separate human being apart from me.

In most of our human relationships, however, we treat people as objects — as an "it." In an "I-It" relationship, I treat you as a means to an end — as I might a toothbrush or a car. I talk to people in order to get something off my chest, not to be with them as separate individuals. I talk about people — authority figures, people in the news, and so on — as if they were subhuman. I get frustrated when people don't conform to my plans or see things the way I do.

The priest and the Levite did not make the connection that emotional maturity (loving well) and loving God are inseparable. They missed the "Thou" lying on the side of the road and simply passed him by.[71]

Question to Consider

Take a few moments to consider the people you will encounter today. What might it look like for you to slow down and treat each one as a "thou" rather than an "it"?

Prayer

> *Lord Jesus Christ, Son of God, have mercy on me. I am aware, Lord, of how often I treat people like an "it." Help me to view each person I meet with the eyes and heart of Christ. In Jesus' name, amen.*

Conclude with Silence (2 minutes)

DAY 4: MORNING/MIDDAY OFFICE

Silence, Stillness, and Centering before God (2 minutes)

Scripture Reading: Luke 7:36 – 39

When one of the Pharisees invited Jesus to have dinner with him, he went to the Pharisee's house and reclined at the table. A woman in that town who lived a sinful life learned that Jesus was eating at the Pharisee's house, so she came there with an alabaster jar of perfume. As she stood behind him at his feet weeping, she began to wet his feet with her tears. Then she wiped them with her hair, kissed them and poured perfume on them.

When the Pharisee who had invited him saw this, he said to himself, "If this man were a prophet, he would know who is touching him and what kind of woman she is — that she is a sinner."

Devotional

The Pharisee did not see the sinful woman as a human being loved by God. He saw a sinner, an interruption, and a person without the right to be at the dinner table. Jesus saw her very differently.

Love springs from awareness. It is only inasmuch as you see someone as he or she really is here and now and not as they are in your memory or your desire or in your imagination or projection that you can truly love them, otherwise it is not the person that you love but the idea that you have formed of this person, or this person as the object of your desire not as he or she is in themselves.

Therefore the first act of love is to see this person or this object, this reality as it truly is. And this involves the enormous discipline of dropping your desires, your prejudices, your memories, your projections, your selective way of looking, a discipline so great that most people would rather plunge headlong into good actions and service than submit to the burning fire of this asceticism.... So the first ingredient of love is to really see the other.

The second ingredient is equally important to see yourself, to ruthlessly flash the light of awareness on your motives, your emotions, your needs, your dishonesty, your self-seeking, your tendency to control and manipulate.

— Anthony De Mello[72]

Question to Consider

What sometimes distracts you from seeing the people you are with as they really are?

Prayer

Lord, I have been forgiven for much more than I will ever realize. Yet I can relate to the Pharisee in this parable. Help me to slow down and be present with you and others so that I might truly see people as you do. In Jesus' name, amen.

Conclude with Silence (2 minutes)

DAY 4: MIDDAY/EVENING OFFICE

Silence, Stillness, and Centering before God (2 minutes)

Scripture Reading: Mark 10:41 – 44

When the ten heard about this, they became indignant with James and John. Jesus called them together and said, "You know that those who are regarded as rulers of the Gentiles lord it over them, and their high officials exercise authority over them. Not so with you. Instead, whoever wants to become great among you must be your servant, and whoever wants to be first must be slave of all."

Devotional

Jesus taught that the kingdom of God is an upside-down kingdom. The disciples kept thinking of the worldly model of power over people rather than Jesus' model of power under — to serve.

It seems easier to be God than to love God, easier to control people than to love people, easier to own life than to love life.

Jesus asks, "Do you love me?" We ask, "Can we sit at your right hand and your left hand in your kingdom?" (Matthew 20:21). Ever since the snake said, "The day you eat of this tree your eyes will be open and you will be like gods, knowing good from evil" (Genesis 3:5), we have been tempted to replace love with power.

Jesus lived that temptation in the most agonizing way from the desert to the cross. The long painful history of the Church is the history of people ever and again tempted to choose power over love, control over the cross, being a leader over being led.

— Henri Nouwen[73]

Question to Consider

What might be one way you can let go of power and control and, in love, choose to serve someone today?

Prayer

Father, you know how much I struggle with trying to love some of the difficult people in my life. I find it easier, like the disciples, to exercise control and have power over people. Fill me with your power so that I can choose to serve, in love, the people I encounter this day. In Jesus' name, amen.

Conclude with Silence (2 minutes)

DAY 5: MORNING/MIDDAY OFFICE

Silence, Stillness, and Centering before God (2 minutes)

Scripture Reading: Matthew 7:1 – 5

"Do not judge, or you too will be judged. For in the same way you judge others, you will be judged, and with the measure you use, it will be measured to you.

"Why do you look at the speck of sawdust in your brother's eye and pay no attention to the plank in your own eye? How can you say to your brother, 'Let me take the speck out of your eye,' when all the time there is a plank in your own eye? You hypocrite, first take the plank out of your own eye, and then you will see clearly to remove the speck from your brother's eye."

Devotional

From the third to the fifth century, the Desert Fathers left a rich deposit of wisdom about how a genuine life with God must lead to a mature, non-judgmental love toward others.

The monk must die to his neighbor and never judge him at all in any way whatever.

If you are occupied with your own faults, you have no time to see those of your neighbor.[74]

Many of us have no trouble at all dispensing advice or pointing out the wrongdoings of others. We don't tend to allow others to be themselves before God or move at their own pace. Instead, we project onto them our own discomfort with their choice to live life differently than we do. The result is that we end up eliminating them in our minds, either trying to make them like us, or falling into a "who cares?" indifference.

Unless I first take the log out of my own eye, knowing that I have huge blind spots, I am dangerous. I must see the extensive damage sin has done to every part of who I am — emotion, intellect, body, will, and spirit — before I can attempt to remove the speck from my brother's eye.

Questions to Consider

Is there someone God is calling you to stop judging? What might it look like to bless and extend mercy to them?

Prayer

Abba Father, forgive me for having so many opinions about so many people and judging them. Wipe my slate clean and give me grace to see my own logs instead of rushing to judge others. In Jesus' name, amen.

Conclude with Silence (2 minutes)

DAY 5: MIDDAY/EVENING OFFICE

Silence, Stillness, and Centering before God (2 minutes)

Scripture Reading: Matthew 10:28, 34 – 36

"Do not be afraid of those who kill the body but cannot kill the soul. Rather, be afraid of the One who can destroy both soul and body in hell.

"Do not suppose that I have come to bring peace to the earth. I did not come to bring peace, but a sword. For I have come to turn

'a man against his father,

a daughter against her mother,

a daughter-in-law against her mother-in-law —

a man's enemies will be the members of his own household.'"

Devotional

Unresolved conflicts are one of the greatest tensions in the lives of Christians today. Most of us hate them. We don't know what to do with them. We prefer to ignore the difficult issues and settle for a false peace, hoping against hope that the issues will somehow go away. They don't, and as a result we end up:

- saying one thing to people's faces and another behind their back.
- making promises we have no intention of keeping, blaming, or becoming sarcastic.
- giving in because we are afraid of not being liked.
- "leaking" out our anger through subtle criticism.
- telling only half of the truth because we can't bear to hurt a friend's feelings.
- saying yes when we mean no.
- avoiding people and giving them the silent treatment.

However, conflict and trouble were central to the mission of Jesus. He disrupted the false peace of his disciples, the crowds, the religious leaders, the Romans, those buying and selling in the Temple, and even in families.

Jesus understood that we cannot build his kingdom on lies and pretense. Only the truth will do.[75]

Question to Consider

Where are you experiencing tension in relationships that you are afraid to disrupt?

Prayer

> *Lord, you know that everything in me wants to run away from tension and conflict, or at least to spin the truth in my favor! Transform my ways of relating to others. Help me to speak the truth with great love and tenderness, and may you be honored and glorified in my relationships. In Jesus' name, amen.*

Conclude with Silence (2 minutes)

The Next Step:
Develop a "Rule of Life"

DAY 1: MORNING/MIDDAY OFFICE

Silence, Stillness, and Centering before God (2 minutes)

Scripture Reading: Daniel 1:3 – 5, 8

Then the king ordered Ashpenaz, chief of his court officials, to bring into the king's service some of the Israelites from the royal family and the nobility — young men without any physical defect, handsome, showing aptitude for every kind of learning, well informed, quick to understand, and qualified to serve in the king's palace. He was to teach them the language and literature of the Babylonians. The king assigned them a daily amount of food and wine from the king's table. They were to be trained for three years, and after that they were to enter the king's service.

But Daniel resolved not to defile himself with the royal food and wine, and he asked the chief official for permission not to defile himself this way.

Devotional

King Nebuchadnezzar and his Babylonian armies conquered Jerusalem and carried off most of the city's inhabitants as slaves. One of those taken was a young teenager named Daniel. Babylon had one simple goal: to eliminate Daniel's distinctiveness as a follower of God and absorb him into the values of their culture — and their gods.

How did Daniel resist the enormous power of Babylon? He was not a cloistered monk living behind walls. He had heavy job responsibilities and many people giving him orders. He had a minimal support system and, I imagine, a very long to-do list each day.

Daniel also had a plan, a "Rule of Life." He did not leave the development of his interior life to chance. He knew what he was up against. While we know little of the specifics, it is clear that he oriented his entire life around loving God. He renounced certain activities, such as eating the king's food (Daniel 1), and engaged in others, such as the Daily Office (Daniel 6). Daniel somehow managed to feed himself spiritually, and he blossomed into an extraordinary man of God — despite his hostile environment.[76]

Question to Consider

What is your plan, in the midst of your busy day, for not leaving the nurturing of your interior life with God to chance?

Prayer

> *Lord, I just need to be with you — for a long time. I can see that there are a lot of things in me that need to change. Show me one small step I can take today to begin to build a life around you. Lord, help me to develop an effective plan in my life for paying attention to you whether I am working, resting, studying, or praying. In Jesus' name, amen.*

Conclude with Silence (2 minutes)

DAY 1: MIDDAY/EVENING OFFICE

Silence, Stillness, and Centering before God (2 minutes)

Scripture Reading: Psalm 73:12 – 17, 25

> This is what the wicked are like —
>> always carefree, they increase in wealth.
> Surely in vain have I kept my heart pure;
>> in vain have I washed my hands in innocence.

All day long I have been plagued;
   I have been punished every morning.
If I had said, "I will speak thus,"
   I would have betrayed this generation to your children.
When I tried to understand all this,
   it was oppressive to me
till I entered the sanctuary of God;
   then I understood their final destiny.
Whom have I in heaven but you?
   And being with you, I desire nothing on earth. (NIV 1984)

Devotional

Christianity is not a set of intellectual beliefs, but a love relationship with God. We need to do what the psalmist did in Psalm 73 — go into the sanctuary of God and be alone with him. This especially applies when we are in the midst of suffering and darkness.

The sayings of the Desert Fathers come from men and women who fled to the desert as a sanctuary to seek God with their whole heart. Eventually, they formed communities around a "Rule of Life." The following are a few of the teachings they left behind. Read them slowly and prayerfully. (A "cell" was an ancient term for a quiet, private place to be with God.)

Abba Anthony said.... "just as fish die if they stay too long out of water, so the monks who loiter outside their cells or pass their time with men of the world lose the intensity of inner peace. So like a fish going towards the sea, we must hurry to reach our cell, for fear that if we delay outside we will lose our interior watchfulness."[77]

Abbot Pastor said: "Any trial whatever that comes to you can be conquered by silence."[78]

A certain brother went to Abbot Moses in Scete, and asked him for a good word. And the elder said to him: "Go, sit in your cell, and your cell will teach you everything."[79]

Question to Consider

How and why do you think finding time alone with God in silence might "teach you everything"?

Prayer

Lord, you know how easily and quickly I lose my interior sense of you. Grant me grace for the rest of today to silence the exterior noises around me so that I would hear the warmth of your voice. In the name of the Father, the Son, and the Holy Spirit, amen.

Conclude with Silence (2 minutes)

DAY 2: MORNING/MIDDAY OFFICE

Silence, Stillness, and Centering before God (2 minutes)

Scripture Reading: Acts 2:42 – 47

They devoted themselves to the apostles' teaching and to the fellowship, to the breaking of bread and to prayer. Everyone was filled with awe at the many wonders and signs performed by the apostles. All the believers were together and had everything in common. They sold property and possessions to give to anyone who had need. Every day they continued to meet together in the temple courts. They broke bread in their homes and ate together with glad and sincere hearts, praising God and enjoying the favor of all the people. And the Lord added to their number daily those who were being saved.

Devotional

My central claim is that we can become like Christ by doing one thing — by following him in the overall style of life he chose for himself. If we have faith in Christ, we must believe that he knew how to live. We can, through faith and grace, become like Christ by practicing the types of activities he engaged in, by arranging our whole lives around the activities he himself practiced in order to remain constantly at home in the fellowship of his Father.

What activities did Jesus practice? Such things as solitude and silence, prayer, simple and sacrificial living, intense study and meditation upon God's Word and God's ways, and service to others. Some of these will certainly be even more necessary to us than they were to him, because of our greater or different need....

... So, if we wish to follow Christ — and to walk in the easy yoke with him — we will have to accept his overall way of life as our way of life totally. Then, and only then, we may reasonably expect to know by experience how easy is the yoke and how light the burden.

— Dallas Willard[80]

Question to Consider

What spoke to you when you read about the lifestyle of the early Christians in Acts and the way they sought to follow the life of Jesus?

Prayer

Lord, you say your yoke is easy and your burden is light (Matthew 11:30), yet the life I live often feels hard and heavy to me. Show me the activities, decisions, priorities, and relationships that are not what you want for me today. I submit my life to your lordship and ways this day. In your name, amen.

Conclude with Silence (2 minutes)

DAY 2: MIDDAY/EVENING OFFICE

Silence, Stillness, and Centering before God (2 minutes)

Scripture Reading: Psalm 63:1 – 5

> You, God, are my God,
>   earnestly I seek you;
> I thirst for you,
>   my whole being longs for you,
> in a dry and parched land
>   where there is no water.
> I have seen you in the sanctuary
>   and beheld your power and your glory.
> Because your love is better than life,
>   my lips will glorify you.
> I will praise you as long as I live,
>   and in your name I will lift up my hands.
> I will be fully satisfied as with the richest of foods;
>   with singing lips my mouth will praise you.

Devotional

Gregory of Nyssa, the great bishop and theologian of the fourth century, argued that there exists in us a ceaseless yearning for God's infinite beauty and splendor. He wrote: "We are led to God by desire. We are drawn upwards towards Him as if by a rope." When the soul glimpses the beauty of God, it yearns to see more. His writings are filled with images describing our longing for God: a lover asking for another kiss, a person tasting a sweetness that can only be satisfied by another taste, the dizziness one experiences standing at the edge of a precipice as one peers into a vast space.

Gregory compares the contemplation of God to a person looking at a spring that bubbles up from the earth:

> As you came near the spring you would marvel, seeing that the water was endless, as it constantly gushed up and poured forth. Yet you could never say that you had seen all the water. How could you see what was still hidden in the bosom of the earth? Hence no matter how long you might stay at the spring, you would always be beginning to see the water.... It is the same with one who fixes his gaze on the infinite beauty of God. It is constantly being discovered anew, and it is always seen as something new and strange in comparison with what the mind has already understood. And as God continues to reveal himself, man continues to wonder; and he never exhausts his desire to see more, since what he is waiting for is always more magnificent, more divine, than all that he has already seen.[81]

Question to Consider

Where can you find the time in your week to "gaze on the infinite beauty of God"?

Prayer

Lord, grant me an even richer glimpse of your infinite beauty and loveliness this day. In Jesus' name, amen.

Conclude with Silence (2 minutes)

DAY 3: MORNING/MIDDAY OFFICE

Silence, Stillness, and Centering before God (2 minutes)

Scripture Reading: 1 Thessalonians 5:16 – 22

Be joyful always; pray continually; give thanks in all circumstances, for this is God's will for you in Christ Jesus.

Do not put out the Spirit's fire; do not treat prophecies with contempt. Test everything. Hold on to the good. Avoid every kind of evil. (NIV 1984)

Devotional

Fire

What makes a fire burn
is space between the logs,
a breathing space.
Too much of a good thing,
too many logs
packed in too tight
can douse the flames
almost as surely
as a pail of water would.

So building fires
requires attention
to the spaces in between,
as much as to the wood.

When we are able to build
open spaces
in the same way
we have learned
to pile on the logs,
then we can come to see how
it is fuel, and absence of the fuel
together, that make fire possible.[82]

Question to Consider

What difference might it make if you were to practice "building open spaces" into your life?

Prayer

> *Lord, I need breathing space. I have too much going on in my life,*
> *too many logs on the fire. Show me the way to create space in my*
> *life, and may the fire of your presence burn in and through me. In*
> *Jesus' name, amen.*

Conclude with Silence (2 minutes)

DAY 3: MIDDAY/EVENING OFFICE

Silence, Stillness, and Centering before God (2 minutes)

Scripture Reading: Psalm 27:3 – 4

> Though an army besiege me,
>   my heart will not fear;
> though war break out against me,
>   even then I will be confident.
> One thing I ask from the LORD,
>   this only do I seek:
> that I may dwell in the house of the LORD
>   all the days of my life,
> to gaze on the beauty of the LORD
>   and to seek him in his temple.

Devotional

The most striking thing about this psalm is what David does when
he finds himself besieged by armies and enemies eager to kill both
him and his family. He does not ask for victory or wisdom or
changed circumstances. Instead, David gets quiet to seek God, to
dwell with him, and to reflect upon his beauty.

163

Each of us needs an opportunity to be alone and silent, or even, indeed, to find space in the day or in the week, just to reflect and to listen to the voice of God that speaks deep within us.... In fact, our search for God is only our response to his search for us. He knocks at our door, but for many people, their lives are too preoccupied for them to be able to hear.

— Cardinal Basil Hume[83]

Question to Consider

In what ways might God be searching for you today — knocking at the door of your life?

Prayer

Lord, a part of me so longs to be alone with you. Another part of me wants to run and avoid time with you at all costs. Thank you for this opportunity today to stop and listen to you. Thank you for continuing to knock at my door — especially when I am too anxious or distant to hear you. Grant to me, I pray, a heart like David's — one that genuinely longs for you above all else in this life. In Jesus' name, amen.

Conclude with Silence (2 minutes)

DAY 4: MORNING/MIDDAY OFFICE

Silence, Stillness, and Centering before God (2 minutes)

Scripture Reading: Psalm 119:27 – 32

Cause me to understand the way of your precepts,
    that I may meditate on your wonderful deeds.
My soul is weary with sorrow;
    strengthen me according to your word.

Keep me from deceitful ways;
    be gracious to me and teach me your law.
I have chosen the way of faithfulness;
    I have set my heart on your laws.
I hold fast to your statutes, LORD;
    do not let me be put to shame.
I run in the path of your commands,
    for you have broadened my understanding.

Devotional

The most famous "Rule of Life" in the Western world is the Rule of St. Benedict, written in the sixth century. In a nonstop, distracted world like ours, a "Rule of Life" brings balance and simplicity, inviting us to a life which seeks everything in proper measure: work, prayer, solitude, and relationships.

Benedict begins his Rule with a call to listen and an invitation to surrender to God:

> Listen carefully, my son, to the master's instructions, and attend to them with the ear of your heart. This is advice from a father who loves you; welcome it, and faithfully put it into practice. The labor of obedience will bring you back to him from whom you had drifted through the sloth of disobedience. This message of mine is for you, then, if you are ready to give up your own will, once and for all, and armed with the strong and noble weapons of obedience to do battle for the true King, Christ the Lord....
>
> Therefore we intend to establish a school for the Lord's service.... Do not be daunted immediately by fear and run away from the road that leads to salvation. It is bound to be narrow at the outset. But as we progress in this way of life and in faith, we shall run on the path of God's commandments, our hearts overflowing with the inexpressible delight of love.[84]

Question to Consider

What would it look like for you to "run on the path of God's commandments"?

Prayer

Lord, you know my world can be nonstop and complex. Help me to balance the demands coming at me today, remembering you while I work, and keeping you at the center of all I do. In Jesus' name, amen.

Conclude with Silence (2 minutes)

DAY 4: MIDDAY/EVENING OFFICE

Silence, Stillness, and Centering before God (2 minutes)

Scripture Reading: Psalm 139:1 – 6

You have searched me, Lord,
  and you know me.
You know when I sit and when I rise;
  you perceive my thoughts from afar.
You discern my going out and my lying down;
  you are familiar with all my ways.
Before a word is on my tongue
  you, Lord, know it completely.
You hem me in behind and before,
  and you lay your hand upon me.
Such knowledge is too wonderful for me,
  too lofty for me to attain.

Devotional

St. Patrick (AD 389 – 461), originally from Britain and raised a Christian, was sold into slavery in Ireland for six years. Upon his escape, he become an ordained bishop and returned to Ireland, traveling widely, evangelizing tirelessly, and organizing churches and monasteries. His mission to Ireland marked an important turning point in the history of missions in the Roman Empire.[85]

Prayer of Saint Patrick

I arise today
Through God's strength to pilot me;
God's might to uphold me,
God's wisdom to guide me,
God's eye to look before me,
God's ear to hear me,
God's word to speak for me,
God's hand to guard me,
God's way to lie before me,
God's shield to protect me,
God's hosts to save me
From snares of the devil,
From temptations of vices,
From every one who desires me ill,
Afar and anear,
Alone or in a multitude....

Christ with me, Christ before me, Christ behind me,
Christ in me, Christ beneath me, Christ above me,
Christ on my right, Christ on my left,
Christ when I lie down, Christ when I sit down,
Christ in the heart of every man who thinks of me,
Christ in the mouth of every man who speaks of me,
Christ in the eye that sees me,
Christ in the ear that hears me.

I arise today
Through a mighty strength, the invocation of the Trinity,
Through a belief in the Threeness,
Through a confession of the Oneness
Of the Creator of creation.[86]

Question to Consider

Which lines from Patrick's prayer speak to you? Carry them in your heart today.

Prayer

Lord, thank you for your reassuring presence that surrounds me. This is almost too wonderful for me to take in! By the Holy Spirit, enlarge my capacity to remain aware of your presence throughout the remainder of this day. In Jesus' name, amen.

Conclude with Silence (2 minutes)

DAY 5: MORNING/MIDDAY OFFICE

Silence, Stillness, and Centering before God (2 minutes)

Scripture Reading: Romans 8:14 – 17

For those who are led by the Spirit of God are children of God. The Spirit you received does not make you slaves, so that you live in fear again; rather, the Spirit you received brought about your adoption to sonship. And by him we cry, "Abba, Father." The Spirit himself testifies with our spirit that we are God's children. Now if we are children, then we are heirs — heirs of God and co-heirs with Christ, if indeed we share in his sufferings in order that we may also share in his glory.

Devotional

Jesus constantly addressed the Almighty, eternal, infinite Yahweh as "Abba," an intimate, warm, familiar word a child would use — not unlike "Daddy." The heart of the gospel is that Jesus gives his disciples the authority to address God as Father. Through Jesus, we too are Abba's child.

Contemplative spirituality moves us along toward a more mature relationship with God. We progress from the "give me, give me, give me" attitude of a small child to a more mature way of relating with God in which we delight in being with him as our "Abba Father." The progression of this movement can be broken down as follows:

- Talking at God: This is simply parroting what our parents or authorities told us to pray. For example, "Bless me, Lord, for these thy gifts, which we are about to receive through Christ our Lord, amen."
- Talking to God: We become more comfortable finding our own words to speak to God, rather than using the ready-made prayers of our childhoods. For example, "Give me, give me, give me more, O God."
- Listening to God: At this point we begin to listen to God, and we begin to enjoy a two-way relationship with him.
- Being with God: Finally, we simply enjoy being in the presence of God — who loves us. This is far more important than any particular activity we might do with him. His presence makes all of life fulfilling.[87]

Question to Consider

What fears are you carrying that you can release to your Abba Father today?

Prayer

Lord, I believe that living a life in your presence is what makes all of life fulfilling. I am just not sure how to get to that point in my spiritual walk. I want to grow beyond a "give me, give me" relationship with you. Fill me with the Holy Spirit so that I might learn to enjoy being with you and stop simply going to you for your gifts and blessings. In Jesus' name, amen.

Conclude with Silence (2 minutes)

DAY 5: MIDDAY/EVENING OFFICE

Silence, Stillness, and Centering before God (2 minutes)

Scripture Reading: 1 John 4:7 – 12

Dear friends, let us love one another, for love comes from God. Everyone who loves has been born of God and knows God. Whoever does not love does not know God, because God is love. This is how God showed his love among us: He sent his one and only Son into the world that we might live through him. This is love: not that we loved God, but that he loved us and sent his Son as an atoning sacrifice for our sins. Dear friends, since God so loved us, we also ought to love one another. No one has ever seen God; but if we love one another, God lives in us and his love is made complete in us.

Devotional

God has a different path for each of us. My closing prayer for you is that you would be faithful to your own path. It is a tragedy to live someone else's life. I know; I did it for years.

I would like to end our time together with a story about Carlo

Carletto. He lived among Muslims in North Africa for ten years with the Little Brothers of Jesus community. He wrote about how, one day, he was traveling by camel in the Sahara desert and came upon about fifty men laboring in the hot sun, trying to repair a road. When Carlo offered them water, to his surprise, he saw his friend Paul, another member of his Christian community.

Paul had been an engineer in Paris — working on the atomic bomb for France. God had called him to leave everything and become a Little Brother in North Africa. At one point, Paul's mother came to Carlo and asked for help understanding her son's life.

"I have made him an engineer," she said. "Why can't he work as an intellectual in the church? Wouldn't that be more useful?"

Paul was content to pray and to disappear for Christ in the Sahara desert. Carlo then went on to ask himself: "What is my place in the great evangelizing work of the Church?" He answered his own question as follows:

> I understood that my place, too, was there, amid the ragged poor, mixing in the mob.
>
> Others in the church would have the task of evangelizing, building, feeding, preaching. The Lord asked me to be a poor man among the poor, a worker among workers....
>
> It's so difficult to judge!...
>
> But to one truth we must always cling desperately — to love!
>
> It's love which justifies our actions; love must initiate all we do. Love is the fulfillment of the law.
>
> If, out of love, Brother Paul has chosen to die on a desert track, by this he is justified.
>
> If, out of love, [others] built schools and hospitals, by this they were justified. If, out of love, Thomas Aquinas spent his life among books, by this he was justified....

I can only say, "Live love, let love invade you. It will never fail to teach you what you must do."[88]

Question to Consider

What might it look like for God's love to invade and fill you, guiding you to what you "must do"?

Prayer

Lord, I can see that there are a lot of things in me that need to change. Let your love invade me. Give me the courage to faithfully follow your unique path for my life — regardless of where it might lead, and regardless of the changes you want to make in me. In Jesus' name, amen.

Conclude with Silence (2 minutes)

Appendix A: The Lord's Prayer

Meditate on each phrase. Take your time; pause after each line.

Our

Father in heaven,

Hallowed be your name.

Your kingdom come.

Your will be done

On earth as it is in heaven.

Give us this day our daily bread.

Forgive us our trespasses

As we forgive those who trespass against us;

And lead us not into temptation,

But deliver us from evil ("the evil one").

Appendix B:
A Guide to Praying the Lord's Prayer

The Lord's Prayer is a masterpiece from the infinite mind of God himself. It has rightly been called one of the greatest gifts of Jesus to us. The following prayer guide was distributed to New Life Fellowship Church as a Daily Office after the sermon series "Learning to Pray: The Lord's Prayer" by Pete Scazzero. These messages can be found online at www.emotionallyhealthy.org.

Our

Thank you, Lord, that you are not simply my Father, but our Father. I thank you that I am part of a worldwide family that is international, intercultural, interracial, intergenerational, and interdenominational, a family that includes all genuine believers who have known you throughout history. Lord, help me to love everyone in this big family of which I am a part. Bless your church around the world.

The Nicene Creed has defined the orthodox Christian faith around the world for over sixteen hundred years. It outlines the boundaries of Christian belief and provides us with a measure for the proper reading of Scripture. Prayerfully reflect on the radical nature of what we believe about our God and the richness of our salvation in Christ, as it is expressed in the Nicene Creed here.

We believe in one God,
> the Father, the Almighty,
> maker of heaven and earth,
> of all that is, seen and unseen.

We believe in one LORD, Jesus Christ,
> the only Son of God,
> eternally begotten of the Father,
> God from God, Light from Light,
> true God from true God,
> begotten, not made,
> of one being with the Father.

Through him all things were made.

For us and for our salvation
> he came down from heaven:
> by the power of the Holy Spirit
> he became incarnate from the Virgin Mary,
> and was made man.

For our sake he was crucified under Pontius Pilate;
> he suffered death and was buried.

On the third day he rose again
> in accordance with the Scriptures;
> he ascended into heaven
> and is seated at the right hand of the Father.

He will come again in glory to judge the living and the dead,
> and his kingdom will have no end.

We believe in the Holy Spirit, the LORD, the giver of life,
> who proceeds from the Father and the Son.

With the Father and the Son he is worshipped and glorified.

He has spoken through the Prophets.

We believe in one holy catholic and apostolic Church.

We acknowledge one baptism for the forgiveness of sins.

We look for the resurrection of the dead,
and the life of the world to come. Amen.

Please note: The phrase "one holy catholic and apostolic church" means "universal" — not the Roman Catholic Church. It refers to the reality that the church of Jesus exists around the world, and not simply in one local church.

Father in Heaven

For you did not receive a spirit that makes you a slave again to fear, but you received the Spirit of sonship. And by him we cry, "Abba, Father." (Romans 8:15 NIV 1984)

Because you are sons, God sent the Spirit of his Son.... So you are no longer a slave, but a son; and since you are a son, God has made you also an heir. (Galatians 4:6 – 7 NIV 1984)

Jesus, I pause now to ponder the miracle that, in your name, I can approach the eternal, infinite God of the universe as "Abba (Daddy) Father." I am in awe, Jesus, that you would give to me your priceless relationship with the Father. Thank you for adopting me, Lord, and for giving me a new core identity as "Abba's child." Your love is beyond human comprehension. Make right all my false ideas of you so that I fall freely into your arms. I receive your infinite love — a love that spurs you to run to me, throw your arms around me, and kiss me (Luke 15:20 – 21). Help me not to fear and to let go of my anxieties and simply be at home with you, Abba.

Hallowed Be Your Name

The greatest need of the world is for people to know you, God, as you really are — that your name be central, not mine. Father, reveal your glory as Abba, that you are close to every human being and truly worthy of our trust. Do this first in me, and then in those around me.

Jesus, you came to reveal God's name as "Abba," cutting through our many wrong perceptions of God. May God's real identity be known to all people. May the whole world (my family, workplace, church, city, nation, and world) have an experience of your infinite love and generosity as Abba. And may your love enable us to trust you — for the good as well as the bad, the successes as well as the failures, the joys and the sorrows. I surrender my fears to you, and I listen to your voice that whispers to me: "All is well, and all will be well." May all the world do the same.

Your Kingdom Come

Lord, may your kingdom come, not mine, nor anyone else's. And may it come first in me and then to those around me. I open up every area of my life to your rule and activity. Father, help me to see the mustard seeds of your kingdom all around me. Teach me to wait patiently for you. Help me, and those around me, not to be discouraged by small beginnings, or to be disheartened because your work seems hidden. Give me eyes to see as you see. May your kingdom come and radically uproot evil — first in me, and then in my family, neighbors, church, workplace, city, governing officials, and the world.

Your Will Be Done (on Earth as It Is in Heaven)

Lord, may your will be done, not mine. And may your will come first in me and then to those around me. You know how easy it is for me to live and forget about your will or desires. Help me, Lord, not to run away from your will as Jonah did. Grant me the courage to faithfully surrender to you. Help me listen to you.

As Thomas Merton prayed:

My Lord God, I have no idea where I am going. I do not see the road ahead of me. I cannot know for certain where it will end. Nor do I really know myself, and the fact that I think I am following your will does not mean that I am actually doing so. But I believe that the desire to please you does in fact please you. And I hope I have that desire in all that I am doing. I hope that I will never do anything apart from that desire. And I know that if I do this you will lead me by the right road, though I may know nothing about it. Therefore I trust you always though I may seem to be lost and in the shadow of death. I will not fear, for you are ever with me, and you will never leave me to face my perils alone.[89]

Give Us This Day Our Daily Bread

Abba Father, I ask for what I need physically to remain alive today. I recognize that everything is a gift from your hand. I also ask you for the spiritual bread I need to do your will today. I am absolutely dependent upon you. You abundantly pour out your gifts to me, yet it is easy for me to take them for granted.

Take a few moments and step back to truly remember where your daily bread comes from — the very hand of God. Pray the following: O God, thank you for the earth, the sky, and the many people whose hard work it is that enables me to enjoy the gift of this bread (food).

Forgive Us Our Trespasses (Debts)

Lord, I have not loved you with my whole heart, mind, soul, and strength. Erase every failure of duty I owe to you and others. I agree with Origen when he wrote: "Suffice it is to say that it is impossible while in this life to be without debt at any hour of night or day." Wipe the slate of my sins clean today. Keep me from being like the Pharisee in Luke 18 who was confident in his own righteousness and looked down on everybody else. Help me to be like the tax collector, and let me humbly pray, "God, have mercy on me, a sinner."

One of the great gifts from the Eastern Church to help us pray is called the Jesus Prayer. Take a few moments to pray this back to God slowly and reflectively, one word at a time:

Lord Jesus Christ, Son of God, have mercy on me, a sinner.

As We Forgive Those Who Trespass (Have Debts) Against Us

Abba Father, you have forgiven me of my enormous debts of sin. You have done so completely and totally — wiping the slate clean. Nonetheless, I struggle to forgive others. I am like the servant in Jesus' parable who, after having been forgiven of his enormous debt, grabs and begins to choke a fellow servant who owes him a very tiny debt (Matthew 18:28).

Lord, grant me a more profound, life-changing experience of your mercy. Teach me to grieve my losses where needed. Break the deeply entrenched chains of sin inside me that desire to get even. Grant me discernment in all of the next steps you have for me. But most importantly, do a miracle within me through the Holy Spirit, so I might be able to extend mercy and bless _____.

And Lead Us Not into Temptation

Father, you know it is difficult for me to stand up under pressure. I acknowledge and agree with your vote of "no confidence" in my ability. I am no match against the evil one without you. Lord, I desperately need you! Strengthen me with your power and grace. I realize that you are bringing events and experiences into my life in order to shape and develop my faith in you, and this growth often revolves around forgiving others. Yet the evil one continually seeks to cut me off in my relationship with you.

Prayer of Preparation:

1. Consider the interactions and activities in front of you today.
2. Remember that you are in an intense spiritual battle with the evil one — who continually seeks to lead you away from God.
3. Remember that God will not let you be tempted beyond what you are able to resist (1 Corinthians 10:13).
4. Pray, "Abba, Father, I am absolutely dependent upon you for power so that I don't give in to temptations. Help me to grow and mature in the challenges I will face today. Amen."

But Deliver Us from Evil (the Evil One)

The great dragon was hurled down — that ancient serpent called the devil, or Satan, who leads the whole world astray.... He is filled with fury, because he knows that his time is short.... Then the dragon was enraged ... and went off to wage war against ... those who keep God's commands and hold fast their testimony about Jesus. (Revelation 12:9, 12c, 17)

Lord, you are right, I have a powerful demonic enemy seeking to lure me into a pit and dominate me. Snatch me from the evil one! Rescue me from Satan's desire to destroy my faith. Help me to discern the temptations of Satan coming at me. Teach me to wait on you when, like Jesus, I am tempted in the wilderness. I place my confidence in you, Father, to care for me today. You speak the truth when you say: "The one who is in you is greater than the one who is in the world" (1 John 4:4). So I affirm with King David: "I will not fear the tens of thousands drawn up against me on every side" (Psalm 3:6 NIV 1984). You are good, and your love endures forever.

Please note: Many of us learned to pray the Lord's Prayer with the following doxology at the end: "For yours is the kingdom, and the power, and the glory, forever and ever. Amen." These words are not found in the Lord's Prayer as taught by Jesus, but it would have been very unusual for a Jewish prayer to have ended without a doxology. It is fine to add this to the prayer when you say it, but remember that Jesus ends the prayer on a surprisingly sober note about spiritual warfare.

Notes

Introduction

1. For a full discussion of the Daily Office, see Peter Scazzero, *Emotionally Healthy Spirituality: Unleash a Revolution in Your Life in Christ* (Nashville: Thomas Nelson, 2006), 153 – 62.

2. Timothy Fry, ed., *RB 1980: The Rule of St. Benedict in English* (Collegeville: Liturgical Press, 1981), 65.

3. The *Emotionally Healthy Spirituality Workbook* comes with a DVD for small groups and classes. It can be ordered online at www.emotionallyhealthy.org.

Week One: **The Problem of Emotionally Unhealthy Spirituality**

4. Quoted in Esther De Waal, *Lost in Wonder: Rediscovering the Spiritual Art of Attentiveness* (Collegeville: Liturgical Press, 2003), 19.

5. Mother Teresa, *A Simple Path* (New York: Ballantine Books, 1995), 7 – 8.

6. Eugene H. Peterson, *Under the Unpredictable Plant: An Exploration in Vocational Holiness* (Grand Rapids: Eerdmans, 1992), 15 – 16.

7. Thomas Merton, *The Wisdom of the Desert: Sayings from the Desert Fathers of the Fourth Century* (Boston: Shambhala, 1960, 2004), 1 – 2, 25 – 26.

8. R. Paul Stephens, *Down-to-Earth Spirituality: Encountering God in the Ordinary, Boring Stuff of Life* (Downers Grove: InterVarsity, 2003), 12.

9. Leighton Ford, *The Attentive Life: Discovering God's Presence in All Things* (Downers Grove: InterVarsity, 2008), 138 – 39, 173.

10. Scazzero, *Emotionally Healthy Spirituality*, 48 – 49.

11. Dan Allender and Tremper Longman III, *The Cry of the Soul* (Dallas: Word, 1994), 24 – 25.

12. Eugene Peterson, *The Contemplative Pastor: Returning to the Art of Spiritual Direction* (Grand Rapids: Eerdmans, 1989), 18 – 19.

13. Scazzero, *Emotionally Healthy Spirituality*, 34.

Week Two: **Know Yourself That You May Know God**

14. Scazzero, *Emotionally Healthy Spirituality*, 80 – 81.

15. Thomas Merton, *New Seeds of Contemplation* (New York: New Directions, 1987), 35.

16. Parker J. Palmer, *Let Your Life Speak: Listening to the Voice of Vocation* (San Francisco: Jossey-Bass, 2000), 10 – 11.

17. Gillian R. Evans, trans., *Bernard of Clairvaux: Selected Works, Classics of Western Spirituality* (Mahwah: Paulist Press, 1987), 47 – 94.

18. Richard J. Foster, *Streams of Living Water: Essential Practices from the Six Great Traditions of Christian Faith* (New York: HarperCollins, 1998), 25 – 32.

19. Henri Nouwen, *The Way of the Heart* (New York: Ballantine Books, 1981), 20.

20. Ibid., 25 – 28.

21. Palmer, *Let Your Life Speak*, 48 – 49.

22. Frederica Mathewes-Green, *First Fruits of Prayer: A Forty-Day Journey through the Canon of St. Andrew* (Brewster: self-published, 2006), xii – xiii.

23. M. Scott Peck, *A World Waiting to Be Born: Civility Rediscovered* (New York: Bantam Books, 1993), 112 – 13.

24. Anthony de Mello, *The Song of the Bird* (New York: Doubleday, 1982), 96.

25. Scazzero, *Emotionally Healthy Spirituality*, 109 – 10.

Week Three: **Going Back in Order to Go Forward**

26. Lori Gordon with Jon Frandsen, *Passage to Intimacy* (Self-Published: Revised Version, 2000), 157 – 58.

27. Thomas Keating, *Intimacy with God: An Introduction to Centering Prayer* (New York: Crossroads, 1996), 82 – 84.

28. John Michael Talbot with Steve Rabey, *The Lessons of Saint Francis: How to Bring Simplicity and Spirituality into Your Daily Life* (New York: Penguin Books, 1998), 246 – 47.

29. Scazzero, *Emotionally Healthy Spirituality*, 111 – 15.

30. Ibid.

31. Quoted in Os Guinness, *The Call: Finding and Fulfilling the Central Purpose of Your Life* (Nashville: Word, 1998), 52.

32. Chaim Potok, *The Chosen* (New York: Ballantine, 1967), 284 – 85.

33. Parker J. Palmer, introduction to *Leading from Within: Poetry That Sustains the Courage to Lead*, by Sam M. Intrator and Megan Scribner (San Francisco: Jossey-Bass, 2007), xxix – xxx.

34. Quoted in Ronald W. Richardson, *Family Ties that Bind: A Self-Help Guide to Change through Family of Origin Therapy* (Bellingham: Self-Counsel Press, 1995), 35.

Week Four: **Journey through the Wall**

35. Michael Harter, S.J., ed., *Hearts on Fire: Praying with Jesuits* (Chicago: Loyola Press, 1993, 2005), 102 – 3.

36. Brian Kolodiejchuk, M.C., ed., *Mother Teresa: Come Be My Light: The Private Writings of the Saint of Calcutta* (New York: Doubleday, 2007), 187, 211, 225.

37. Ibid., 215.

38. Scazzero, *Emotionally Healthy Spirituality*, 122 – 23.

39. Thomas Merton, *The Ascent to Truth* (New York: Harcourt Brace and Co., 1951), 188 – 89.

40. Wayne Muller, *Sabbath: Finding Rest, Renewal, and Delight in Our Busy Lives* (New York: Bantam, 1999), 187 – 88.

41. Richard Rohr with Joseph Martos, *From Wild Man to Wise Man: Reflections on Male Spirituality* (Cincinnati: St. Anthony Messenger Press, 1990, 1996, 2005), 2.

42. Peter Scazzero, *The Emotionally Healthy Church* (Grand Rapids: Zondervan, 2003), 167.

43. Henri Nouwen, *In the Name of Jesus: Reflections on Christian Leadership* (New York: Crossroads Publishing, 1991), 62 – 64.

44. Oswald Chambers, *My Utmost for His Highest*, ed. James Reimann (Grand Rapids: RBC Ministries, 1935, 1992), devotion for July 29.

Week Five: **Enlarge Your Soul through Grief and Loss**

45. Nicholas Wolterstorff, *Lament for a Son* (Grand Rapids: Eerdmans, 1987), 81.

46. Scazzero, *Emotionally Healthy Spirituality*, 136.

47. Gerald L. Sittser, *A Grace Disguised: How the Soul Grows through Loss* (Grand Rapids: Zondervan, 1995), 39, 44, 61 (cf. p. 37).

48. Joni Eareckson Tada and Steven Estes, *When God Weeps: Why Our Sufferings Matter to the Almighty* (Grand Rapids: Zondervan, 1997), 135 – 36.

49. *http://www.atthewell.com/itiswell/index.php*.

50. Parker Palmer, *Let Your Life Speak: Listening for the Voice of Vocation* (San Francisco: Jossey-Bass, 2000), 98 – 99.

51. Scazzero, *Emotionally Healthy Spirituality*, 148 – 49.

52. Eugene Peterson, *Leap Over a Wall: Earthly Spirituality for Everyday Christians* (New York: HarperCollins, 1997), 120 – 21.

53. Ken Gire, *The Weathering Grace of God: The Beauty God Brings from Life's Upheavals* (Ann Arbor: Vine Books: Servant Publications, 2001), 96–98.

54. Scazzero, *Emotionally Healthy Church*, 161–62.

55. Scazzero, *Emotionally Healthy Spirituality*, 151–52.

Week Six: **Discover the Rhythms of the Daily Office and Sabbath**

56. Merton, *New Seeds of Contemplation*, 14–15.

57. Scazzero, *Emotionally Healthy Spirituality*, 156, 155.

58. Ibid., 161.

59. Thomas Merton, *Confessions of a Guilty Bystander* (New York: Doubleday, 1966), 86.

60. Thomas Merton, *Contemplative Prayer* (New York: Doubleday, Image Books, 1996), 29–30.

61. Wayne Muller, *Sabbath: Finding Rest, Renewal, and Delight in Our Busy Lives* (New York: Bantam Books, 1999), 69.

62. Ibid., 82–85.

63. Norman Wirzba, *Living the Sabbath: Discovering the Rhythm of Rest and Delight* (Grand Rapids: Brazos, 2006), 22–24.

64. Lynne M. Baab, *Sabbath Keeping: Finding Freedom in the Rhythms of Rest* (Downers Grove: InterVarsity, 2005), 17–19.

65. Eugene H. Peterson, *Working the Angles: The Shape of Pastoral Integrity* (Grand Rapids: Eerdmans, 1987), 49.

Week Seven: **Grow into an Emotionally Mature Adult**

66. Scazzero, *Emotionally Healthy Spirituality*, 193.

67. Ibid., 179–80.

68. Henri Nouwen, *Return of the Prodigal Son: A Meditation on Fathers, Brothers, and Sons* (New York: Doubleday, 1992), 17.

69. David G. Benner, *Sacred Companions: The Gift of Spiritual Friendship and Direction* (Downers Grove: InterVarsity, 2002), 47.

70. Michael Collopy, *Works of Love Are Works of Peace: Mother Teresa of Calcutta and the Missionaries of Charity* (San Francisco: Ignatius, 1996), 35.

71. Scazzero, *Emotionally Healthy Spirituality*, 181–83. I also recommend Malcolm Muggeridge, *Something Beautiful for God* (New York: Harper & Row, Image Edition, 1971), 119.

72. Anthony De Mello, *The Way to Love: The Last Meditations of Anthony De Mello* (New York: Doubleday, Image Books, 1995), 131–32.

73. Henri Nouwen, *In the Name of Jesus*, 59 – 60.

74. Quoted in Rowan Williams, *Where God Happens: Discovering Christ in One Another* (Boston: Shambhala, 2005), 14.

75. For a full discussion, see Scazzero, *Emotionally Healthy Spirituality*, 184 – 93.

76. Scazzero, *Emotionally Healthy Spirituality*, 197 – 98.

Week Eight: The Next Step: Develop a "Rule of Life"

77. Benedicta Ward, *The Sayings of the Desert Fathers* (Kalamazoo: Cistercian, 1975), 3.

78. Merton, *Wisdom of the Desert*, 122.

79. Ibid., 44.

80. Dallas Willard, *Spirit of the Disciplines: Understanding How God Changes Lives* (San Francisco: Harper & Row, 1988), ix, 8.

81. Quoted in Robert Louis Wilken, *The Spirit of Early Christian Thought: Seeking the Face of God* (New Haven: Yale University Press, 2003), 302.

82. Judy Brown, "Fire." Widely available on the internet; see, e.g., www.judysorum brown.com/blog/breathing-space. Used by permission.

83. Cited in Esther De Waal, *Lost in Wonder: Rediscovering the Spiritual Art of Attentiveness* (Collegeville: Liturgical Press, 2003), 21.

84. Timothy Fry, *Rule of St. Benedict 1980*, 15, 18 – 19.

85. Dale T. Irvin and Scott W. Sunquist, *History of the World Christian Movement: Volume 1: Earliest Christianity to 1453* (Maryknoll: Orbis Books, 2001), 236 – 37.

86. Adapted from the version of Patrick's famous prayer found at: www.ewtn.com/Devotionals/prayers/patrick.htm

87. Mark E. Thibodeaux, *Armchair Mystic: Easing into Contemplative Prayer* (Cincinnati: St. Anthony's Press, 2001), chapter 2.

88. Carlo Caretto, *Letters from the Desert, anniversary edition* (Maryknoll: Orbis Books, 1972, 2002), 108, 100, 23.

Appendix B: A Guide to Praying the Lord's Prayer

89. Thomas Merton, *Thoughts in Solitude* (New York: Farrar, Straus & Cudahy, 1956, 1958), 169.

Emotionally Healthy Spirituality Day by Day

A 40-Day Journey with the Daily Office

Pete Scazzero

In this groundbreaking devotional book, Peter Scazzero introduces the ancient spiritual discipline of the Daily Office. The basic premise of the Daily Office is simple: We need to intentionally stop to be with God more than once a day so that practicing the presence of God becomes real in our lives.

Each day offers two Daily Offices — Morning/Midday and Midday/Evening — where each pause can last from five to twenty minutes.

Available in stores and online!

Emotionally Healthy Spirituality Course Workbook *and* Emotionally Healthy Spirituality Course: A DVD Study

It's Impossible to be Spiritually Mature, While Remaining Emotionally Immature

Peter and Geri Scazzero

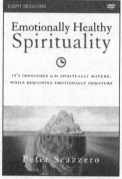

For those desiring to take steps in their Christian life and discipleship, to break free from bondage to the past and experience healing, *Emotionally Healthy Spirituality Course* is an eight-session, video-based Bible study on the integration of emotional health and contemplative spirituality. Many sincere followers of Christ, followers who are passionate for God, join a church, participate weekly in a small group, serve with their gifts, and are considered "mature," remain stuck at a level of spiritual immaturity — especially when faced with interpersonal conflicts and crises. The *Emotionally Healthy Spirituality Course* video study and companion study guide offer a strategy for discipleship that address this void, offering powerful pathways to transformation that will help people mature into a faith filled with authenticity and a profound love for God.

The eight sessions include:

1. The Problem of Emotionally Unhealthy Spirituality
2. Know Yourself That You May Know God
3. Going Back in Order to Go Forward
4. Journey through the Wall
5. Enlarge Your Soul through Grief and Loss
6. Discover the Rhythms of the Daily Office and Sabbath
7. Grow into an Emotionally Healthy Adult
8. Go to the Next Step to Develop a "Rule of Life"

The Emotionally Healthy Church, Expanded Edition

A Strategy for Discipleship That Actually Changes Lives

Peter L. Scazzero with Warren Bird

The Emotionally Healthy Church, Updated and Expanded Edition, features a fuller, deeper look at the six principles contained in the original and includes a crucial, additional chapter: Slow Down to Lead with Integrity. New Life Fellowship in Queens, New York, had it all: powerful teaching, dynamic ministries, an impressive growth rate, and a vision to do great works for God. Things looked good—but beneath the surface, circumstances were more than just brewing. They were about to boil over, forcing Peter Scazzero to confront needs in his church and himself that went deeper than he'd ever imagined. What he learned about the vital link between emotional health, relational depth, and spiritual maturity can shed new light on painful problems in your own church. In this revised and expanded edition of his Gold Medallion Award-winning book and groundbreaking bestseller, Scazzero reveals exactly how the truth can and does make you free—not just superficially, but deep down. You'll acquire knowledge and tools that can help you and others:

- look beneath the surface of problems
- break the power of past wounds, failures, sins, and circumstances
- live a life of brokenness and vulnerability
- recognize and honor personal limitations and boundaries
- embrace grief and loss
- make incarnation your model to love others
- slow down to lead with integrity

The Emotionally Healthy Church, Updated and Expanded Edition, includes story after story of people at New Life whose lives have been changed by the concepts in this book.

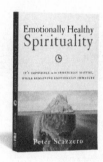 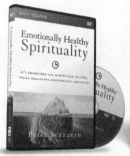 

For more information on implementing
Emotionally Healthy Spirituality and
Emotionally Healthy Spirituality Day by Day
into your life, small group, or church, go to:

www.emotionallyhealthy.org